THE GLORY OF

Isaiah 43:2

Jo Barron Hardy

Copyright © 2014 Jo Barron Hardy.

All rights reserved. No part of this book may be used or reproduced by any means, graphic, electronic, or mechanical, including photocopying, recording, taping or by any information storage retrieval system without the written permission of the publisher except in the case of brief quotations embodied in critical articles and reviews.

Scripture quotations are from The Holy Bible, English Standard Version® (ESV®), copyright © 2001 by Crossway, a publishing ministry of Good News Publishers. Used by permission. All rights reserved.

Scriptures taken from the Holy Bible, New International Version®, NIV®. Copyright © 1973, 1978, 1984, 2011 by Biblica, Inc.™ Used by permission of Zondervan. All rights reserved worldwide. www.zondervan.com The "NIV" and "New International Version" are trademarks registered in the United States Patent and Trademark Office by Biblica, Inc.™

Scripture taken from the King James Version of the Bible.

Inspiring Voices books may be ordered through booksellers or by contacting:

Inspiring Voices
1663 Liberty Drive
Bloomington, IN 47403
www.inspiringvoices.com
1 (866) 697-5313

Because of the dynamic nature of the Internet, any web addresses or links contained in this book may have changed since publication and may no longer be valid. The views expressed in this work are solely those of the author and do not necessarily reflect the views of the publisher, and the publisher hereby disclaims any responsibility for them.

Any people depicted in stock imagery provided by Thinkstock are models, and such images are being used for illustrative purposes only. Certain stock imagery © Thinkstock.

ISBN: 978-1-4624-0798-9 (sc)
ISBN: 978-1-4624-0799-6 (e)
Library of Congress Control Number: 2013919342

Printed in the United States of America.

Inspiring Voices rev. date: 1/8/2014

Dedication

This book is dedicated to ALL whose
lives have been interrupted
by the fierce blow of someone
they loved and trusted,
and to the
Almighty Father
who steps in and saves.

Introduction

Sunday August 28th, 2011

Oh how I wish I could finish this book. The story is written in my mind and on my heart forever. It has made me so much of who I am today. But every time I come back to work on it, it takes me to a place I really do not want to return. My life today and the past few years have been days of peace and quiet. Coming back here drags me to days of fear and darkness. A place I don't want to go or remember. So today I put it away again, possibly for good… or possibly to pick back up again. I would love to have the courage to finish it because it has a great ending with a new beginning, the Glory of Hope.

January 2012

A dream awoke me… God was speaking to me. He was urging me to write… to tell **HIS** story, through mine. The story He wants told.

February 2013

Writing this book, reliving a past I would rather forget, took me back to a place I never thought I would go. Yes, so many times I tried to start again and always stopped. I suppose I knew the inevitable was lurking around the corner. And my fears became truth. I did as had done so many years earlier. I withdrew. Shame over came. I made excuses. I became weak, irritable, and isolated. I could no longer see my real life and what was before me, only what was behind me, a deep, dark cloud of despair and of hopelessness.

I guess in a way I hit rock bottom. I was ravaged by fear, shame, and regret. I sought help. In spite of my flaws and failures, I am loved.

I am far from perfect; yet perfectly loved.

And above all, our Heavenly Father, who no matter what we are, who we are, why we are and how we are, we are, always His.

Matthew 10:28
"The only one you should fear is the one who can destroy the soul." (NCV)

Dear Readers, I hope you can excuse any text errors that may be in this book. It is not flawless. I hope you can read this with an open heart and accept the book as it is. Just as our Lord accepts us.

Acknowledgement

I have so many to thank for getting me through the writing of this book.

To family and friends who have shown deep devoted love, support, encouragement and acceptance.

Special thanks to Roy and Don for their daily inspirational and motivating emails. To LeAnne who always seems to recognize when I need, and how to get a good belly laugh out of me. To my life long friend Mary Helen who has inspired me for years to just believe. To my dear friend Christy who always allows me daily doses of who she is. To my emotional "coach" Kitty, for picking me up out of the rubble and helping me to believe in myself again. To my friends, Denise, Arch IV, and uncle Don who stepped in and volunteered their skills of editing, a huge task.

And a very special thanks to my uncle Roy for allowing me to use his spectacular photo for the cover. For it is a photo revealing hope, a ray of light through darkness.

Jeremiah

33:3

"*Pray to me,
and I will answer you.*" (NCV)

Contents

Chapter 1	"you formed me"	1
Chapter 2	"God will comfort"	9
Chapter 3	"you are the giver of life"	13
Chapter 4	"you will have trouble"	17
Chapter 5	"foolish taking root"	25
Chapter 6	"give thanks in all"	31
Chapter 7	"my God will hear me"	35
Chapter 8	"I have good plans for you"	39
Chapter 9	"do not fear, I will help you"	51
Chapter 10	"floods cannot drown love"	59
Chapter 11	"but wisdom is better"	63
Chapter 12	"he is mighty to save"	65
Chapter 13	"Lord watch over you"	67
Chapter 14	"he who guards you"	69
Chapter 15	"great glory that will be shown"	79
Chapter 16	"he gathers them like lambs"	83
Chapter 17	"my place of safety"	91
Chapter 18	"I will guide you"	99
Chapter 19	"he will himself restore you"	105
Chapter 20	"thanks be to God"	113

Chapter 1

Year 1990

"You made my whole being: you formed me in my mother's body" (NCV)
Psalm 139:13

"Bye guys! I love you!" Bess pulled the seat belt tight around her. That was fun she thought. Riding around with her buddy Lynn, looking at houses. They always had so much fun together and the thought of buying a home was exhilarating.

Bess walked in the door of her apartment, tossed her mail on her desk and went to her bedroom to change. She was still in her office clothes and the thought of slipping into her pajamas relaxed her thoughts instantly. She glanced at her answering machine. Four messages, ugh, I am not returning four phone calls tonight. It was 10:30 PM anyway. She punched the play button and the calls were rattled off. "What was that one?" she said out loud. "Vanderbilt Hospital!" Has something happened to Bright? Bess knew her best friend in Nashville daughter had been in the hospital several days before, but she couldn't understand the hospital calling her about that. Those thoughts rushed through her head as she began dialing the number left on her machine.

"Yes this is Bess Clay; I had a message on my answering machine to call."

"Yes Ms. Clay, is your mother Meredith Clay?"

"Yes," Bess answered, she was beginning to tremble.

"Ms. Clay, we have been trying to reach you, please wait on the line for the doctor."

"Ms. Clay, this is Dr. Kennedy, your mother has been involved in an auto accident," he hesitated, "her injuries were fatal." Bess heard nothing more. He body became rigid and the room began to spin. Fatal, she thought. Doesn't he know fatal means death, it does, doesn't it? Bess doubted herself. She started to ask the doctor the same question, when she heard him say the man that was with her is here.

"A man was with her?" she asked.

"Yes," the doctor told her.

Bess responded quickly, "May I talk with him?"

"I will get him," the doctor replied.

The silence was chilling. Bess was on the verge of screaming Mom, when she heard Patrick's voice on the phone; he was saying, "Bess I am so sorry your mother has passed away." Patrick and her mom had been dating for some time. Bess heard the words, but could only think; where am I? Patrick began to sob. Bess quickly regained her thoughts.

"Patrick, please, it's not your fault, please, are you okay?" Numbly, almost unaware, Patrick and Bess began to discuss immediate plans. No one had been able to get in touch with Bess's two brothers. Her younger brother lived close to Nashville, where her mother lived, and her older brother lived out of state. "I will try to get in touch with them," Bess said. Patrick was going to stay at the hospital until Bess arrived. She was three hours away.

Bess dialed her younger brother's number, but could not get through. She dialed her older brother in North Carolina. Her sister-in-law answered. Through tears Bess asked to speak to her brother. You've got to be strong, she told herself. Alex came on the line.

"Hey Sis, what's up?" Alex, like her, was always upbeat. Bess was three years younger than her older brother and less than 18 months older than her younger brother. They both loved her; she was very athletic and challenged them both on occasion.

"Alex, it's Mom, she's been in an auto accident," and Bess, choked not knowing how to tell him, "She was killed."

"What?" she heard the word, but more than that she heard the confusion and shock.

"She died, Alex."

Their mother had been broadsided. She was the passenger in her own car, Patrick had been driving. It was a freak accident. A car merging from the interstate at a high rate of speed, lost control, jumped a guard rail and landed in their mothers lap crushing her chest. She had to be cut out of the vehicle. She was given three tanks of oxygen as they tried to save her. She died on the way to the hospital. The medics told Bess later at the hospital that Meredith was trying to say something. What? Bess thought. That she loved her children? Bess was sure of it. Meredith Clay's children and her grand-children were the brightest part of her life.

On the way back home Bess recounted the past week's events. She had arrived at the hospital in Nashville around 2:00 AM. Her younger brother Keith was there along with Patrick, and her mother's brothers and sister. She listened to the doctors explain what had happened, and how they had tried to save her. Bess hugged and spoke with her aunt and uncle. She asked to see her mother, but was told she couldn't.

Her mother had donated her eyes and inner ears, and those had already been taken. They would not allow Bess to see her mother that way. Her mother had also requested to have her remains be sent on to medical research. There was some discussion about the arrangements and eventually Bess and Keith went home with Patrick and discussed the accident. Bess's mother was just learning to play golf and Patrick was helping her. They had been home from work and were on their way to the driving range to practice before dinner. Bess was aware of everything that was happening but she was numb, deafly numb. Leaving Patrick, Bess went to her mother's condo. It was going on 5:00 AM by then. Bess tried to close her eyes but the ache was starting to set in.

All of a sudden everything was different. There was nothing but empty space, no beginning, no end, no color and no sound. My very best friend is gone; my mother is gone. The one person in the world I could always count on. Her love never faltered, she was always there for me, strong and solid. I can still feel her hug Bess thought as she drifted off.

Bess, her two brothers at her side, walked down the aisle. The church was standing room only. They had been out front greeting the guests for 30 minutes and now that everyone was seated it was their turn to join the family, friends and guests who loved and admired their mother. It was a huge loss for so many people. Bess sat down by her youngest niece. Grandma was a big force in Joslyn's life and Bess knew this was going to be very hard for her to accept. At a very young age Joslyn's parents had divorced and now only two years later she had lost her grandmother. Bess put her arms around Joslyn and kissed her forehead and told her she loved her.

The memorial service was touching and sweet. Bess had found a poem in her mother's wallet and knew it must have meant a lot to her. The pastor read the poem and also read a poem that Alex had written years earlier about the strength of love. She was our anchor Bess thought how will we make it without her? As she pulled Joslyn close to her Bess closed her eyes and felt the familiar arms of her mother around her as tears flowed down her cheeks.

After the memorial service they all went to the clubhouse of the condo community where her mother had lived. Food had been brought in and Bess visited with the many guests, dreading the task that lay ahead of sorting through her mother's things. The tasks that lay ahead of them seemed endless and Bess sat down feeling lost and exhausted.

By the end of the week most things had been taken care of. Bess's uncle, her mother's youngest brother was the executor of her will and the trustee of her estate as well as the grandchildren's trusts. Earlier in the week Bess had planned to load up a small U-Haul and take the items that she was keeping home with her, but by Friday she just couldn't deal with it. She left the things in her mother's condo, rented a car and began the drive home. The drive was a lonely one.

Bess turned the key in the door to her apartment. As she stepped inside it seemed like a decade since she had gotten the news of her mother's death, but at least she was home. She phoned a few friends, got caught up on the events she had missed, ran a hot bubble bath and fell into bed gasping from the sobs.

Chapter 2

"Those who are sad now are happy, because God will comfort them." (NCV)
Matthew 5:4

"This is it! This is it right here! This is the one I want right here!" Bess was practically jumping up and down and waving her arms as if things might disappear before her very eyes. She turned to watch Micah, her builder, tromp through the thick brush.

"You're sure?" he asked as he caught up with her and gazed into her blue eyes.

"Yes," she commanded and then followed with "You don't think there are ticks that live here do you?" as she winked at Micah and walked ahead. "Seriously Micah," Bess said with the look of a child, "I just have this vision of you and me on the job site, hard hats on, plans splayed across the hood of your truck, heads together discussing options."

"Yea?" Micah said, "You've been watching too much TV."

"Yea," Bess squints back at him.

"I'll get you a hard hat," said Micah, "a pink one." Bess sent him a challenging look, and they both laughed.

While waiting in the realtor's office Bess paced. "He's late" Bess announced, slightly annoyed. Although she really wasn't. Micah's and her relationship had blossomed into something very special. Nothing romantic, more like a brother and sister, and they teased each other about it often.

"He's here," Elise said looking out the front door of the real estate office as Bess approached her.

"Why is he parking in the north forty?" Bess chided.

"He loves his truck," Elise said amused. Bess knew that was true and she loved to pick at Micah about it, to the point of getting on his nerves.

Micah, Elise, and Bess went over the house plans, the building costs and some add on's. After about an hour of hounding Micah, Bess had her way. They would start clearing the land next week. Bess was out there every day watching the progress of what was to be her new home. The guys that worked for Micah looked forward to seeing her pull up. They had become her buddies.

Bess showed up on Saturday mornings with hot coffee and donuts. She bought the men a boombox just because she figured they liked country music and would like to hear something other than the hammering and drilling. She was out early one morning walking around her yard and walked right into a two by four that was a support for the porch. Bess fell flat on her back. As much as they loved her, the builders could not stop laughing long enough to help her up. Once she finally got to her feet and highly embarrassed, she went about her surveying as if nothing had happened, chuckling just a bit inside. Bess loved her life and the gifts God had blessed her with.

"What color brick do you want for the foundation?" Micah asked.

"I don't know," Bess shrugged.

"Okay," Micah said rolling his eyes. "What color roof?"

Bess answered, "I don't know."

"Have you considered exterior paint color?"

"Well, not really," Bess responded.

"Get in the truck," Micah commanded.

"Why?" Bess asked.

"We're going for a ride."

"Where to?" Bess asked as she climbed into the truck.

"Shopping," said Micah, as he climbed in beside her. Micah then headed to some nearby neighborhoods that were more developed. As he took Bess from house to house they discussed everything from brick color to landscaping. By the time they were done, all the decisions had been made. They teased each other and laughed the whole time.

Finally, there it stood the house that Bess had built. It was the prettiest house in the neighborhood, as she had heard repeated often. She felt like putting a plaque on the wall by the front door saying, "In loving memory of my Mother". Bess could not have accomplished this without the funds her mother had left her from her estate. It was a gift and a blessing to honor her mother.

It had only been seven months since her mother's death and although Bess still missed her mother dearly she had reached a point of peace. There was no gravesite to visit, no headstone to look at, but Bess understood her mother's wishes and respected the fact that she had chosen cremation over the traditional burial services. She knew her mother was in Heaven handling some very important job for God. She was there with her parents, Bess's father, grandparents and various other family and friends she had lost during her life. As she stood back and looked at her home, Bess said a silent prayer and thanked God and reminded her mother of how much she loved her.

Chapter 3

"You are the giver of life" (NCV)
Psalm 36:9

"Elise, can you recommend a mover?" Bess asked.

"Well as a matter of fact I can," Elise replied. "Call me at the office tomorrow and I will look up the name and contact information."

Bess checked the time, and mumbled to herself, that mover guy is late. She was waiting on the owner of the moving company to give her an estimate. It was only August and her house would not be ready until October, but she wanted to know what her expenses would be and have a solid budget to stick to. The knock on the door startled her.

The owner introduced himself, "I'm Cole Green." He had a strong handshake and was quite polite. He made a quick walk through her one bedroom apartment, looking in closets and cabinets, but only after asking first. Summing everything up he announced, "Well this is nothing!" Bess thought to herself, taking his comment personally, well it may be nothing to you mister but it's everything to me. Then she quickly remembered to mention the items she had in storage, much of which had belonged to one of her parents or grandparents. They settled on a price that Bess thought seemed reasonable.

Cole started down her apartment steps and stopped to ask her if she was married. "No," Bess replied. "I am not."

"I'm married to the road," he replied; as he bounced down the steps. As Cole climbed into his moving truck he turned to his buddy who was waiting on him and said confidently, "Sold," and as he started the engine he added, "I'm going to marry that girl."

On the closing day, Micah, Elise, and Bess sat in the office of the title company. Bess signed page after page after page of closing documents. It was done. The house was hers. The many trips she had made from Harleysville to Owltown, every weekday and Saturdays. Watching the progress; Bess was finally able to realize her life-long dream. From a vacant lot full of trees to a yard with a house, it was now her home. Bess couldn't help but smile. Thank you mom, I love you, she sighed.

The Glory of Hope

The movers did a great job. Neither a scratch nor dent in the walls or the furniture, and it was a beautiful fall day. Cole had called her a few times since she had met him at her apartment. He was fun to talk to and really sweet and they had talked about going out. He wrote up her bill and she handed him a check and he said, "I'll spend it all back on you."

After the movers left, Bess went and let her cats Patch and Eddie out of their kennels. She picked each one up and held them close to her chest and loved them. Thanking God for all the good things he had done for her. And now there was this charming man who seemed intoxicated by her. Good things come out of bad she told herself.

She took Patch and Eddie and showed them each room, the garage, then the back deck, talking out loud to each of them. She explained it all to them as if they understood every word. Looking out over the back yard, she held Eddie tight in her arms and said, "This is your new big back yard, look at all the trees you can climb." Bess laughed to herself. She knew Eddie was far too lazy and plump to make an attempt.

Chapter 4

"in this world you will have trouble" (NCV)
John 16:33

Cole arrived to pick Bess up for their first date in a new Cadillac he had rented just for the occasion. Bess answered the door and let him in. She assessed him quickly and smiled to herself. His wardrobe appeared to be brand new. Bess got her coat and they walked out. The cold November wind hit her face and she shivered. Cole put his arm around her to warm her. What a gentleman Bess thought as he opened the car door for her. They went to an R&B lounge and had a glass of wine and danced, and then on to a country joint. Cole said he wanted to take her to dinner at this catfish diner on the river near his apartment. Bess happily agreed. The food was good and the view of the river was beautiful. Bess was enjoying herself and Cole said he wanted to take her to his apartment to meet someone. Bess felt perfectly comfortable with him and agreed to go. Cole turned the key to his apartment and let her in. Bounding down the hallway was a darling cocker spaniel. "Oh, he is so cute." Bess gushed. She bent down to pet the dog and he sat happy and content to be the object of her affection.

"That's Tagg." Cole introduced.

"He's so sweet," Bess said, "cockers are my favorite."

Cole showed Bess around his apartment. He had a huge pool table in the living room. He grabbed a couple of beers out of the fridge and they shot pool and laughed and played with Tagg. It was getting late and Bess knew she had had enough to drink. The drive from Cole's place to Bess's was a long one and Bess suggested they go.

Cole came inside when they got back to Bess's house. It was chilly in the house when they walked in and Bess suggested building a fire. Cole went to work and before long the room was warming. They sat down on the floor in front of the fire and talked until early in the morning. Cole reached over and pulled Bess's face to his and kissed her gently. Bess kissed him back and before she knew it she was swept into his arms. She almost melted at the feel of Cole's strong arms around her. She could hardly catch her breath as she pushed her body close to his. "Let's go to the bedroom," Bess whispered. Cole hesitated; he didn't want to indulge her on the first date, although his need for her was overpowering. He picked her up and took her to bed, where they made love. They fell asleep in each others arms.

Cole woke before dawn and woke Bess, apologizing for having to wake her so early. It was a Saturday morning, a day off for her, but Cole's busiest day. Bess followed him to the door and felt sorry for him as he left for having to get up so early and working on a Saturday. Yawning, Bess headed back to bed. She pulled the covers around her shoulders and drifted back to sleep, thinking of nothing but Cole. She knew she couldn't sleep long. She had a long day ahead and she was cooking dinner for some friends.

Bess was busy in the kitchen when the phone rang; she wiped her hands and answered. "Bess, this is Mindy." Mindy worked for Cole, and before Bess could greet her, Mindy had begun. "I know Cole was out all night last night and I know he rented a new Cadillac for his date, or suspect he did, that's what he does when he wants to impress someone."

"Why are you telling me this?" Bess asked.

"Cole and I have lived together for the past two years," Mindy replied. "My parents keep urging me to leave him because they say he is no good, but Cole belongs to me. He's a violent person Bess; there are holes in the wall all over our apartment. I'm just telling this to you Bess for your own good. You're better off to stay away from him." Bess was alarmed, she had no idea Mindy and Cole had any ties other than she was an employee of his. Mindy continued on her crusade and Bess had enough. She thanked Mindy for the phone call and hung up. She immediately dialed Cole's number and got his answering machine. Bess tried to seem calm and just asked that Cole please call her when he got in.

Bess was quick to get back to work but just could not get the conversation she had with Mindy out of her mind. She was going to end it with him. Although it had only begun, Bess felt a tug at her heart and a little sadness. She really liked Cole and the way he treated her. She felt like a princess when she was with him, but she reminded herself, she didn't need or want any trouble. She wasn't sure about Cole, but she was sure Mindy could be trouble.

Bess's guests arrived right on time and she met them with huge hugs. Bess was glad to see them and after the day she had, she needed to be close to her good friends. Jim and Lynn were always there for her; they were two of her biggest fans. Bess pulled out beers for everyone and they retreated to the den to sit and chat. They had just sat down to eat when the phone rang. Bess picked up the cordless; it was

Cole. She glanced at Jim and Lynn and told them to go ahead, that she would be right back. She took the phone to the bedroom to speak to Cole. Cole was in a good mood and it was obvious he was happy she had called. "Cole, thank you for last night, I really appreciate it, but I will not be seeing you again," she said.

Cole feeling the rejection and not understanding why, objected, "Bess, what's wrong, did I do something wrong?"

Bess did not want to get into the conversation that she and Mindy had. "No Cole, it's not you, it's me."

"Have you just had a change of heart?" Cole asked. Bess felt they were talking as if they were breaking off an engagement. And she had guests waiting and needed to end their conversation.

"Yes," Bess answered, "I just had a change of heart." Cole hung up reluctantly, and was furious on the other end of the line.

Cole slammed the door behind him as he walked across the hall from his apartment to Harry's place, Cole's business manager. Cole pounded on the door, Harry answered. "Mindy's done it again." Cole shouted, barely able to keep from picking up something and throwing it.

"Done what?" Harry asked halfway irritated. Both he and Cole had just gotten in and Cole worked a person hard. Cole's energy level was huge and trying to keep up with him was exhausting and Cole expected his employees to keep up with him. He paid his employees well and was very generous to their needs, but he also demanded a lot.

"She's gotten to Bess." Cole said exasperated as he sat down, head down with his shoulders stooped. Harry's heart went out to Cole. He always seemed to get the bad breaks and really was a good person.

"What do you mean, Cole?" Harry asked again. "What has Mindy done?" Cole and Mindy had been on again off again for a couple of years. Their relationship wasn't love, at least for Cole, but need, and quite stormy at times. Cole had not stopped talking about Bess all day and Harry was glad to see his friend and boss so happy. But now, it was as if the air had been let out of him. Cole was about six feet tall and the best built and strongest man Harry had ever met. Deep inside that tough, burly exterior was a heart of gold, laced with a lot of anger and pain.

Harry sat down beside his friend. "Bess called and said she didn't want to see me again." Cole blurted.

"Why?" Harry asked, "I thought you guys had a great time last night."

"And now she doesn't want to see me again." Cole said.

"Do you want me to call her?" Harry offered. "I'll talk to her, I'll find out what happened."

"Thanks Harry." Cole said while walking back to his apartment.

The phone rang as Bess and Lynn were cleaning up from dinner. It was Harry and he re-introduced himself to Bess, having only met her during her move. Bess retreated to her bedroom for the second time that evening. Harry told her that Cole was disappointed and upset and tried unsuccessfully to pull out of Bess what had happened. Harry went into more detail of Cole and Mindy's relationship trying to alleviate her doubts, but not pushing her too hard. Harry assured her that Cole knew nothing of him calling her and Bess finally gave in and confided that, yes, Mindy had called her. Harry talked with Bess for a moment and told her he knew this was her decision, but asked her to reconsider. Cole seemed to be crazy about her and he felt the two of them deserved a chance.

Bess thanked Harry, hung up and went back to the kitchen. "You okay?" Lynn asked, "Anything going on?" Lynn knew her friend and could read her well.

"No," Bess replied, "nothing at all." But Bess had a lot on her mind.

Shortly after Lynn and Jim left, Bess called Cole. He seemed very sad and she felt her heart go out to him. Cole asked her to drive over and although she hesitated, she eventually gave in. It was late when she reached Cole's apartment but was glad to see him. Cole felt he owed Bess an explanation about Mindy and Bess listened to a story of a rocky relationship with no real love involved. Bess was quick to understand and told him as much. They talked for a while longer, but both were tired and fatigued from the day's events. It had been a long, busy, and stressful day for both of them. They quickly fell asleep.

Chapter 5

"I have seen the foolish take root" (KJV)
Job 5:3

Bess and Cole's love affair heightened right away. Away from work, they were inseparable. Soon, they were falling in love.

Cole was such a kid at heart and loved to shower Bess with flowers and gifts, which he did well. They spent their first Christmas together at Cole's apartment with what Bess referred to as Cole's frat brothers. Cole cooked and as usual the food was excellent. They had dinner and spent the evening shooting pool with Cole's buddies. The time came for presents. Cole handed Bess a nicely wrapped box and Bess opened it and inside was a Bart Simpson sweat shirt. Cole loved the Simpsons, Bess tolerated that relationship, and Cole knew Bess couldn't stand the cartoon, or the characters. Bess pulled the sweat shirt out of the box with a not so excited look and glared at Cole. Cole just laughed at her for a while and finally said, "Take a look at Bart's eyes." Bess looked closer and gasped. Pinned to the sweat shirt in Bart's eyes were a set of half carat diamond earrings. Bess let out a little squeal and jumped up and down.

"Oh my gosh Cole, they're beautiful!" Bess hugged Cole hard and thanked him. "I can't believe you did that," laughing now. She had never had a gift like that before from a man.

Bess was spending many nights at Cole's. She would come in from work and Cole would have a bubble bath run for her, and sweet notes waiting for her. Bess had insisted she needed thirty minutes of quiet time when she got home from work and Cole made sure this happened for her. After all, it was like a frat house at Cole's every night with his buddies there shooting pool. Cole had also begun buying Bess teddy bears. It was a tradition of some sort to him, and Bess soon had a collection going.

Bess agreed to join Cole on a Florida trip in early February. Traveling by a 26 foot moving van was new to Bess, but Cole knew all the tricks of long road traveling and he made sure Bess was comfortable and had everything that she needed. She enjoyed the trip and her time with Cole. She had not spent so much time with a man in quite sometime and she loved it and the way Cole obviously loved her. They finally made their way to their destination in Florida after several stops on the way down dropping off and picking up furniture. Cole had rented a nice cottage on the beach for them. Bess spent time there while Cole worked. He would come in early and spend late afternoons with her. They soon became friends with a white heron that would eat from their hands. They lounged lazily in the sun and talked softly and dozed peacefully; to Bess it was Heaven.

When it was time for Bess and Cole to head back home and their routine lives, she did not want to leave. Her life with Cole seemed like a fairy tale, and she didn't want reality to set back in. Bess and Cole strolled hand-in-hand on the beach the last night. The air was warm and the moon bright. She could feel something different with Cole tonight. Cole stopped and reached for her. "Will you marry me?" he said.

Bess, without thought, answered. "Yes, I love you!" the only words she could say.

The next day Bess bought a postcard and sent it to her friends at her office, telling them of her spectacular trip with Cole. She rambled on and said goodbye, then added a P.S. Cole and I are engaged!

Bess arrived at her office after the postcard had brought her good news. Bess felt an air of reluctance in her friends and co-workers. They just obviously weren't as thrilled as she was. But she assured herself, they didn't know Cole the way she did. Once they did, they would love him with the same great intensity as she did. As the days went by Bess called friends and relatives and told them of her news. Bess insisted she knew what she was doing even though she had not known Cole that long, she knew him well. They set a wedding date in April. That only gave Bess a couple of months to plan and prepare; so she went at it full speed. She made phone calls and appointments and soon had the church and her pastor lined up. Lea, her pastor, and Bess were fairly close. He had counseled her through the death of her mother. Lea knew Bess but he didn't know Cole and he intended to get to know him. The theme of the wedding was roses and Bess picked out a wedding band of rosebuds, her bouquet was roses and the cake would be decorated with roses. Bess and a friend drove to Atlanta and she found the perfect dress. It was antique white lace over satin. The sleeves were long lace and the bodice had jewels that hung from it. It was quite 1880's and flattered Bess's small figure and height. Cole and his ushers would wear white and burgundy.

Cole moved into Bess's house in late March. His rent was up and they both saw no reason for Cole to sign another rental lease. Besides, they would be married in less than a month.

Cole was working and Bess was unpacking some of Cole's things. She ran across a box with some legal documents in it. She looked closer and realized she was holding divorce papers between Cole and a woman named Wanda. Cole had told Bess about Wanda sometime before, but he never mentioned they were married. He had told her that it was a very rocky relationship and drug related. Cole had been arrested a year earlier for possession of cocaine for resale, but as he had explained to Bess, he was buying it to support Wanda's habit and got busted; he said he was set up. Bess didn't want to intrude on Cole's past and privacy but as she was refolding the papers, something caught her eye.

Cruel and inhumane treatment, "Typical grounds," Bess said out loud, but she read on. Wanda had accused Cole of outrageous, violent acts of anger. Throwing dishes, china, pictures, art, anything he could get his hands on. He was accused of yelling foul language and of hitting her. Bess was suddenly aware of how still she was and that she wasn't breathing. Bess read over the paragraph and went to call Cole. She felt she had to confront him, although she knew there could be no truth to any of it.

Although Bess was on the other end of the phone line, she could feel Cole's anger. He wasn't angry at her or accusing because she had read the papers. He was angry that his past was coming back to haunt him yet once again, although none of it was his fault. "She made all that up Bess; you know I would never do something like that. If you're having second thoughts, tell me about it and we will call the whole thing off right now." Cole was yelling and Bess wished she had never approached him about it.

"Cole, it's okay, I believe you, and I understand. I'm sorry, okay? Just finish your job up and hurry home. I miss you and I love you."

Bess picked the papers up again and was tempted to read them again, then quickly folded them and put them back in the box and onto a shelf in the top of the closet. She went to the kitchen to start dinner but could not shake the uneasy feeling growing inside her.

Chapter 6

"give thanks in all circumstances, for this is God's will for you in Christ Jesus" (NIV)
1 Thessalonians 5:18

The wedding rehearsal was on a Friday night with the wedding on Saturday afternoon. Bess and Cole had friends and family coming from Birmingham, Nashville, Charlotte, and Evansville. Bess's favorite uncle was giving her away. Maggie Ann, her best friend since the third grade, was her Maid of Honor. Everything seemed to be in place. They all went through rehearsal then back to Bess's house to open gifts. They all had a great time but Cole seemed to be drinking more than usual. He was staying with friends at a nearby hotel and when it came time for everybody to leave, Cole insisted on driving. It was obvious to all that he had no business driving, even if it was just backing out the driveway. It took the whole crowd to convince Cole not to drive. He was such a big strong man that no one wanted to get in his way. Cole would never admit that he had a weakness. With much coaxing Cole relented and allowed someone else to drive.

The next morning Maggie Ann and Bess awoke early, had coffee and a light breakfast and then were off to have their hair and nails done. Then off to the church to do their makeup and get dressed and do some photos. Maggie Ann and Bess were enjoying themselves and Bess being at the back of the church getting ready, had no idea ten minutes before the wedding was to begin that Cole was not there.

Maggie Ann hugged her friend of thirty years and wished her the best. She did not have a good feeling about her friend's choice of a husband, but she didn't mention it and pushed those feelings to the back of her mind. This is her wedding day Maggie Ann thought and I want it to be the best possible day. She and Bess dressed and did their makeup amid laughter, giddy chatter and reminiscing. All the guests had arrived. No one alerted Bess, but Cole was nowhere to be found.

Angry, Cole scoffed, "I'm going to be late for my own wedding. Get out of the way you jerk," he yelled as he pushed the accelerator to the floor. The speedometer read 100 as he raced down the interstate to the church. Thankfully, he was already dressed. The pianist was playing as Cole rushed into the church and was met by his ushers, best man and Lea their pastor. Lea breathed a sign of relief and was glad that they could get started. Lea had known Bess for a couple of years now and he loved her. It was Cole that bothered him. He just didn't feel comfortable with this union.

The bride's march started and Bess found herself walking down the aisle. The music was beautiful, but Bess could only think of Cole and how much she loved him and that this was the beginning of her new life, and how wonderful it all was going to be.

The preacher asked them to join hands. Cole held Bess's hands tightly as he looked into her eyes. He was so much in love and never wanted to be away from her. He thanked God for her everyday. Now he was being asked if he took her to be his wife. Instead of "I do," Cole replied, "With every breath I take."

They kissed and practically ran down the aisle of the church. They were so in love and now all they could think about was getting to the mountain chalet they had rented and spending the next few days alone.

Chapter 7

"But as for me, I watch in hope for the Lord, I wait for God my savior; my God will hear me." (NIV)
Micah 7:7

Bess yawned and stretched as she awoke, and she smiled as she smelled the fire slowly burning out. The chalet she had picked out was amazing. The bedroom was a loft with a wood burning fireplace. There was a hot tub on the deck looking out over the mountains, and Bess and Cole soaked there the night before beneath the stars. There were no other houses in sight. They loved the privacy and laughed until they couldn't walk as they ran through the frigid mountain air back into the chalet and made love more than once that night.

Cole stirred and Bess snuggled close to him. His body felt warm and firm. I guess he will always have an incredible body, Bess thought. Cole turned to face her and again they made love. Bess was starting to drift back to sleep when Cole nudged her, "Are you hungry?" he asked. Bess smiled, remembering the groceries they had bought when they got to the mountains, and how she had complained at the outrageous prices.

"Starving," Bess replied as she flung her arms around him and kissed him hard.

"Good," he said, "I'll let you know when it's ready."

Bess lounged for a few minutes thinking how lucky she was to have such a wonderful man in her life. She could smell the aroma of breakfast and decided it was time to rise. She slipped out of bed and put on the robe Cole had bought for her. He had bought her the most beautiful robe and gown as a wedding gift. It was the prettiest thing she had ever seen, and it amazingly resembled her wedding gown.

Downstairs, Cole had fixed her a Bloody Mary along with a grand breakfast of bacon, omelets and biscuits. Cole was a fabulous cook, among other things… Bess thought.

The mountain air was crisp and refreshing. It was early spring and the nights were still quite chilly. There was even a light snowfall one night. Cole and Bess lounged and walked around the town of Gatlinburg shopping, sightseeing and eating at their favorite places. They even managed a little putt-putt contest. Time flew by and it was time to head back home. Bess was regretful but Cole seemed to be getting a little restless.

After they arrived back home from the honeymoon, Cole seemed to be a little agitated and Bess couldn't understand why. He checked his messages immediately when they got home and told her there was a problem on a job site and he would have to go help out. Bess didn't want the honeymoon to end, but she said she understood and sadly watched him pull out of the driveway. She turned to all the wedding gifts and decided they needed to be put away. That will keep me busy, Bess thought, until Cole gets back.

Chapter 8

*"I have good plans for you, not plans to hurt you.
I will give you hope and a good future." (NCV)*
Jeremiah 29:11

Bess and Cole combined their dog and cat families in her small house in Owltown. Eddie and Patch reluctantly accepted Tagg into the household. Tagg was a sweet dog and Bess had always been fond of cockers. It was one of the things that had attracted her to Cole.

Bess wanted to make sure Tagg was up on all his shots and that he was in good health. She took him to her vet for a visit. Through an x-ray, a large mass was revealed on one of Tagg's lungs. The vet thought that it needed to be removed and Bess and Cole decided that they would take Tagg to the University of Tennessee Animal Hospital for surgery. They left early one Friday morning for the appointment in Knoxville.

Tagg was taken back while Bess and Cole waited. Bess left to get them some coffee and as she was returning she heard Cole yell for her. She rushed back and there was a doctor explaining to Cole that Tagg's heart had stopped and that the tumor was attached to his heart as well as the lung. The doctor said they had been massaging Tagg's heart for several minutes with no response and asked for permission to stop. Bess said "No, keep trying." The doctor left and Bess and Cole were left sitting in shock. Twenty minutes later the doctor was back stating that they were having no luck in resuscitating Tagg. Reluctantly, Bess and Cole agreed to let them stop. The doctors prepared Taggs body for Bess and Cole to take back with them.

Bess and Cole cried the entire trip back home. Neither of them said a word. They were both so stunned that they couldn't speak. Bess felt so terrible for Cole. She knew how much Tagg meant to him and they had been together for many years.

When they got home Cole dug a grave for Tagg. Cole was sobbing and let out a few curse words. He told Tagg, that he had always been there for him, and he loved him dearly. Bess and Cole had a death in their family and it was so very painful.

Although the house was small for them and their family had grown to six animals, it was all they needed. Cole wanted to put in a swimming pool but

Bess couldn't see spending the money and besides it was way too much work. They were putting in many hours with the business and Cole was on the road quite a bit. But his persistence paid off and they had an above-ground pool installed with decking all around. Cole had been right; it was great fun to have.

Bess was working full time for an insurance firm and trying to help Cole with his moving business. Bess was starting to get calls at her office about moving jobs and when she arrived at home from the office it seemed work just went from one desk to the other; from hers at the agency to Coles. It was starting to be too much for her. She felt bad that one job was interfering with the other. She felt she wasn't doing a good job with either. Nothing was getting her full attention. Bess finally confronted Cole with it and expressed her frustration and desire to help him and devote her time to his business. Cole laughed at her lovingly. "I just think you're burnt out on insurance Bess," he said. "Whatever you do babe is okay with me."

Bess was both nervous and excited at this prospect of change. She had a well paying job with great benefits, but she was completely convinced that what her husband was doing had great potential and she believed in him. She had never helped run a company before and knew nothing about it. But she believed she had made the right decision. Besides, she had a small nest egg put aside and if this didn't work out she could always go back to the business she left.

Cole was up and out early as Bess sat down at her desk. Across the hall she thought, is our bedroom. This is pretty cool she thought, as she went to the kitchen to make a pot of coffee. "Now what do I do?" she said out load.

Soon, Bess was getting the hang of it. She was learning how to schedule jobs and have the manpower and equipment available. As Bess got more involved, she did whatever it took to get the job done. And the more that meant being on jobsites, the more she realized just how good Cole was at what he did and the relationship he had with his clients. He was the best, Bess observed, now let's make this company the best.

Cole was adamant about appearance and pleasing the client. He was making a name for himself and Bess was soaking it all in. Cole seemed to be a magician at times. There wasn't anything he couldn't figure out. Bess marveled and she forgot nothing.

Bess was reading books, making contacts and working on a branding image. Cole had been renting Budget trucks, subletting storage space and working employees as sub-contractors. He was not paying taxes or making transportation filings. None of this sat well with Bess and now was the time to take it on. She made the proper filings for hauling for hire. She bought insurance for the company and began withholding taxes on their employees. Bess was learning as she went along and loving it. Cole often barked at her, "I wish we were still doing business out of a Red Food bag."

Cole fought Bess on everything but he always gave in. Although he didn't want to pay the dues, he knew what Bess was doing was making his name grow beyond anything he could imagine and he was grateful.

One of the biggest projects Bess took on was developing a logo for the company as well as a brochure. "We need something the public can recognize," she told Cole, "and something you can place in someone's hand that says who we are."

Bess was obsessed with these ideas. She rolled ideas over and over in her head. She worked with a friend of hers that owned her own public relations firm. Cole had always told Bess stories about his father who was a salesman for Steinway pianos. "He was always top salesman," Cole would brag, "and I started helping him move pianos when I was nine years old." This kept rolling over and over in Bess's mind. Cole seemed to be so proud of that. Laughingly, Bess sketched the outline of a young boy pulling a red wagon loaded down with a baby grand piano. With that, the public relations firm went to work. A couple of weeks later Bess presented her logo to Cole. "My God," Cole scoffed, "no way." But, Bess was persistent. She ordered yard signs, business cards, brochures and letterhead; everything the company used and needed had the new logo of the little boy pulling the red wagon loaded with a baby grand piano. Cole tolerated it, but inside he loved it; he just didn't want to admit it.

Soon he was everywhere, the little boy pulling the red wagon loaded with a baby grand. That was Cole. Business was booming. Bess and Cole formed a corporation and Cole made the ownership 50/50 split with Bess. They truly were a team. It wasn't long before Cole purchased a company-owned truck. He had it custom-built the way he felt would work best for his company's needs. On each side of the truck was the little boy pulling the red wagon with the baby grand piano.

With the addition of company-owned trucks and employees, Bess wanted to take the office out of their home. She found some empty warehouse space with about 15,000 square feet for a reasonable price. They would have to build it out for their needs but by now Bess was confident with their abilities to make things work best for their company. Once Bess had a plan on paper for the layout for warehouse space

The Glory of Hope

and office, she presented it to Cole and he went with her to discuss it with the building owner. Once they agreed on what could be done and a price, they hired a contractor and the build-out began. After several weeks, Bess and Cole were moving into their new office and warehouse.

The first day Bess arrived for work at their new place was exciting for her. When she pulled up, the trucks were running and crews getting ready to pull out. Bess was filled with joy and pride as she looked at the sign on their side of the building. We've come a long way baby, she thought!

Cole started looking at cocker puppies. He missed Tagg terribly and loved cockers. At last he found one through an ad in the paper. It was a three month-old-male. Bess wasn't really ready to get another dog, but knew how badly Cole missed Tagg. He had even accused her of killing him in a fit of grief, but Bess knew he didn't mean it. Cole was away on a trip and Bess called the owner of the puppy again and asked if she could come see it. She did and she quickly fell in love. The puppy ran around, gnawed and was constantly untying Bess's shoes. She was laughing, and the puppy was licking as she left with him. It was going to be Cole's Valentine present. Bess was going to surprise him when he came home. But when Cole called that night, she couldn't help herself and spilled the beans. Cole was excited and ready to get home and see his new buddy. His name was Archie. Patch and Eddie had a new puppy to contend with!

The phone rang and Bess recognized the number on the caller ID. It was the Monte's, Cole's best friend in another state. Big Cash was Cole's lifetime friend. Cole loved and admired Cash as much as any person Bess had seen. Cash's wife Rachael was a good friend to Cole as well. Bess answered and Rachael's question startled her. "Where is Cole, Bess?"

"He's out on a job. Rachael, is something wrong?"

"It's Cash. Bess, he passed away last night." Bess caught her breath. She wasn't quite sure what to say.

"Rachael, oh my, what happened?"

Cash had died in his sleep. Bess told Rachael how sorry she was. Rachael wanted to be the one to break the news to Cole, and Bess agreed. As she hung up the phone in tears, she knew this would break Cole's heart. The afternoon was a long one as Bess waited for Cole to come home.

Cole arrived home earlier than usual. Bess told him that Rachael wanted him to call her. Bess watched the expression on Cole's face as he talked with Rachael and saw the anguish and tears in his eyes. Cole hung up the phone, looked at Bess and only said, "not Cash." He went to the sofa, sat down and wept.

The Glory of Hope

Bess and Cole quickly made friends with their neighbors; especially Jack and Becky. They had all met at a neighborhood block party. Bess and Cole and Jack and Becky spent many week nights and weekends together. Champagne and munchies were their favorite. There were kids' birthday parties, adult birthday parties, and holidays all celebrated together.

One Easter afternoon, Cole and Jack went out on some secret expedition. Bess was hanging out with Becky and the kids. Cole and Jack pulled back in the driveway, got out of the truck and headed toward the house. Looking out the window it was obvious to Bess that Cole was cradling something small in his arms.

"Happy Easter babe," Cole announced, and he held out a snow white baby bunny with red eyes.

"Cole, what do you think we are going to do with that?" Bess snapped. By now they already had three dogs and three cats. That was enough.

"She's for you babe," Cole answered.

"Oh, thanks, honey," Bess replied, and took the tiny bunny from Cole. "She's sweet and so soft." Bess had a real soft spot for anything with fur. But she sure didn't need another mouth to feed; and, where would they keep her, didn't rabbits require a cage? Later Cole explained to Bess that the bunny for her was just a front. Jack actually wanted the bunny for his kids, but knew Becky would protest. This way Bess could protest and Becky would give in to a homeless cute, bunny. Backfire… as it turned out Jack and Becky's daughter was quite allergic to rabbits. Bess had a new bunny.

Bess and Cole loved entertaining. They often invited friends and employees over for poolside parties and playing pool basketball. Archie loved the water and would jump in and go after the basketball as the adults shot hoops. They had snacks, grilled burgers, talked and laughed. Everyone always went home full, happy and exhausted. Cole treated his friends and employees very well.

Their first Christmas in the little house was full of joy. Bess decorated and Cole did most of the cooking. They had friends over and exchanged gifts and laughter. With a fire going, Bess and Cole settled in for Christmas night. They each exchanged a gift and went to bed early. The next morning Cole fixed breakfast and they opened the remaining gifts. Cole told Bess, "You're missing one!"

"Where?" Bess smiled at him. He was always up to tricks and loved surprises.

"Take a look at the tree; check it out Bess." Bess rose and walked to the tree.

"Look up," said Cole. She searched and searched but couldn't find anything. Cole walked over and

The Glory of Hope

gently pulled out a diamond tennis bracelet, hanging from one of the branches.

Bess eyes widened, "Cole, it is beautiful." Bess was truly taken aback. The bracelet was beautiful and nothing she would have ever gotten for herself. He hung it in the tree. Of course he did she thought, as she hugged and thanked him. Christmas was her favorite time of year and this had certainly been a special one.

Chapter 9

"For I am the Lord, your God, who takes hold of your right hand and says to you, do not fear; I will help you." (NIV)
Isaiah 41:13

The following fall, Bess and Cole took a long trip in the moving truck on a north route up to Washington State and back down the California 101, and back home on a southern route. They were gone two weeks and had the cockers with them. On the way, they stopped in St. Paul to visit with their friends Jack and Becky who had moved a few months earlier. Although it was fall, St Paul had not had snowfall yet, but that didn't stop Cole and Jack from getting out the snow mobiles and flying around like two kids on Jack and Becky's property. The trip down the California 101 was breath taking. They stopped about every 50 miles or so to catch the beautiful view of the Pacific coast.

On one stop the weather would be warm, a few miles later; it would be quite chilly. They stopped and had lunch at the Big Sur.

When they finally made it back home they were all pretty pooped. They had spent many hours every day in the moving truck with the dogs and sleeping in hotels. It had been a great trip, and a profitable one but they were all ready to be back in their own home and own beds.

Cole threw a birthday party for Bess. He had their neighborhood friends over and several of the guys that worked for them. They had snacks and cake. They shot pool in the garage and Bess opened gifts. Cole had put up all kinds of decorations and had balloons everywhere. They all had a great time and the party went late into the night.

The next day Bess and Cole were in their home office working, they were discussing their upcoming schedule, both in town and out of state, and putting crews together for each. Cole pretty much ran the scheduling, crews and jobs. Bess handled the taxes, state filings, insurance, and incoming mail. Cole hated being in the office and it was beginning to show that morning. Bess snapped at him about something and before she knew what was happening, Cole slammed her face down into her desk; her eye and lip catching the stapler. He marched out of the house. Bess raised

The Glory of Hope

her head in disbelief, asking herself, what had just happened? Cole soon came back and apologized to her, asking her for forgiveness. He said didn't mean to hurt her and he was very sorry. Bess said, "That's okay," and walked away.

The next day, their neighbor Becky came over. She immediately asked Bess what had happened. Bess was sporting a nice shiner. She made up a story that she was cleaning up after the party, retrieving a balloon from behind the TV, and had hit her eye on the TV, remarking how clumsy she had always been.

Bess and Cole were at home and going over some last minute details for the upcoming week's schedule. Cole had put some grease on the stove to cook and came back to join Bess in their home office. Bess was busy and not aware that Cole had grease cooking on the stove, but smelled an odor. Both Bess and Cole took off for the kitchen. The grease was flaming and Bess quickly dumped a canister of flour on the flames. This only made the fire ignite more. Flames shot up and caught the overhead cabinets on fire. Cole picked up the flaming pot and headed to the back door, but the pot was too hot and Cole had to set it down on the floor. Bess got the back door opened and Cole tried it again. He got to the door but couldn't hold on any longer and tossed the pot and flaming grease across the deck.

"Cole, are you okay?" Bess asked, reaching for him.

"Yes," Cole answered.

Bess looked down and Archie stood between them. His white fur was singed from the hot grease. "Oh my gosh, Archie!" Bess bent down to make sure he was okay. Bess loved on him reassuringly. The cabinets above the stove were burned, a place in the floor was burned, and the deck suffered some damage but humans and animals were okay. Bess was grateful.

Several weeks later, Cole and Bess lounged together watching the Tennessee -Alabama football game on TV. It was a huge rivalry for both teams and Cole was a huge Alabama fan, and Bess a huge Tennessee fan. The night was fun and Bess and Cole did well, especially because Cole's Alabama team won. Bess was a good sport even though her team had been beaten. After the game, Cole was in the kitchen working on dinner. Bess walked in and hugged her husband. Cole turned to her and they kissed. Bess said, "Let's make love," and a shadow crossed Cole's face. Immediately he was furious.

"The only reason you want to make love is because Alabama won." Cole knew what he meant, but Bess had no idea. Cole became wild. Bess tried to explain to him that it had nothing to do with the game, but he was relentless. Bess went from room to room trying to talk to him and avoid him at the same time to no avail. As each moment went by Cole became more out of control.

Bess went to their office to try and do some paper work to get away from Cole. Cole followed her; furious she had something on her mind other than him. As Bess thumbed through some papers, Cole turned the desk over on top of her. She winced at the pain on the top of her legs and pushed back but eventually had to pull herself out from underneath the desk. She ran to the kitchen and dialed 911. When they answered she hung up. Before she could walk away from the phone it rang. It was 911 calling her back. "Is there a problem?" someone asked on the other end.

"No," Bess answered trying to sound calm.

"You made a call to us," was the response. "Is anything wrong?"

"No," Bess answered again, starting to cry.

"It doesn't sound like it," the operator pressed.

"I'm fine," Bess said, "and I'm really sorry to have bothered you."

Cole had heard the conversation and was hounding her, "Who was that?"

Bess replied, "I made a phone call I shouldn't have, but it's okay now. I have taken care of everything."

Cole followed her to the bath off their bedroom. Bess just wanted him to go to sleep. He seemed drunk.

But as they got closer to the bathroom Cole started to push and shove her. She went into the bathroom, brushed her teeth and washed her face, and came out to find Cole defiant in her path.

Bess had just about had enough of Cole's out bursts of anger, his hitting, throwing furniture and damaging the walls of her house. Her temper started to boil and she opened the door and tried to walk past Cole. He shoved her into the dresser. She turned to him and in hatred she spat at him, "If you want to beat the life out of me, just go ahead and do it." Bess felt the first of his fists on her face. Then it was one after the other after the other. Cole kept swinging. Bess fell to the floor and tried to scramble out of Cole's reach. Cole started kicking along with hitting. Bess covered her head and curled into a ball. Soon everything went black.

Bess slowly and painfully raised her head. She didn't know where she was. Her face and all the rest of her body hurt. She reached up with one arm and felt the side of her bed. Slowly, she pulled herself up and rolled onto the bed. She passed out again, but not before she remembered that night.

When Bess woke, she felt so fragile. She tried to stretch but her body ached. She rolled over and over in her head and could tell in her subconscious that Cole was not there. Finally, she stood and walked to the bathroom. She looked at her reflection and she fell backward. What she saw engulfed her whole body, mind, and soul. Her face was swollen and she was black and blue all over. Both eyes were black and she had bruises down her neck and arms and legs. This really happened, she thought, I am really looking at me. She thought of what was inside her and who she was and she found nothing. Bess was hollow. She stood there alone, staring at her reflection. The room seemed to spin but she couldn't look away. It seemed as though she were in a movie, in someone else's body, in someone else's life. She continued to look at herself until reality came back to her and yes she was looking at herself.

She walked slowly back to her bed and sat down. Still in shock, but also knowing she had to do something, she knew she couldn't do this alone.

Chapter 10

"even much water cannot put out the flame of love, floods cannot drown love" (NCV)
Song of Solomon 8:7

She dialed the number. By now Bess was starting to shake. "Bax, it's me, Cole has beaten me up, please come I need your help." Baxter was on his way.

Bess and Baxter had dated for about a year and half. And loved each other still, they were good friends.

Bess got up and went to the den. Still so lost as to what had happened. No feelings surfaced, only sheer emptiness. Baxter arrived and Bess clung to him. Baxter couldn't bear to look at her but he took charge. He called Bess's friend Elise. Baxter explained to her what had happened. Elise told him she was on her way. Baxter stayed with Bess, holding her, until Elise arrived.

Baxter answered the door, Bess stood back in the shadows. He thanked Elise for coming and told Bess he would be calling her. Elise began to weep as she folded her friend into her arms and led her to the couch. They wept together as they held each other. "He's sick," Elise said, pushing her friend away from her and forcing her to look into Bess's eyes. "He's sick Bess." Elise asked Bess if there was someone she could call and Bess replied yes, Lea. Lea was the associate pastor at the church that Bess and Cole attended. He had baptized Cole just before they had gotten married and had performed their wedding ceremony. It was after church hours and Elise got ahold of Lea on the first try. "Is her jaw broken?" Lea asked. Elise hadn't even thought of that but answered, "no, I don't think so." Elise and Lea talked for a short while and both agreed, even though Cole was out of town, Bess needed to be taken out of there.

Bess and Elise talked for a few minutes and Elise got up and asked Bess to pack a bag. "Why?" Bess asked.

"I'm taking you out of here," Elise replied.

"Elise, I can't leave," Bess argued, "I have the pets to take care of. Cole's out of town. I will be fine here."

"No," Elise said, "you are coming with me."

The following day Elise took Bess to the hospital to have her injuries checked and to file a police report.

While in the emergency room she was asked if she had been in a car accident, and she looked down and only responded "I wish it was that simple." She was examined by the doctor and nothing was broken. The police came and made a report and asked Bess if she wanted to press charges and she said, "No."

Bess stayed with Elise a couple of days and then against Elise's wishes, but at Bess's request, she took her back home. Bess argued that the pets needed her and that she didn't want Cole to think that he had won. After all, this was her home and she was not going to give in to Cole's anger and fits of rage to keep her away.

Bess was home when Cole arrived. They had already spoken on the phone and Bess had asked him to move out. He had one of his crew help him pack up a few items. Cole was moving into a trailer not too far away. Even though it was hard for him to face Bess and the bruises, he insisted that it was her fault, that she had provoked him. Bess questioned herself.

Bess knew her Heavenly Father and knew that the only way for their marriage to recover was through the grace and strength of God. She bought Cole a Bible and left it in his mail box along with a note. It seemed to touch Cole and over the next few weeks Bess and Cole reconciled and Bess allowed him to move back home.

They both were glad to be back together and happy. A tremendous amount of damage had been done, but they both seemed committed to getting their marriage back on track.

Chapter 11

*"wisdom is better, because it can
save whoever has it" (NCV)*
Ecclesiastes 7:12

Things were never the same between Bess and Cole. Cole's anger seemed to increase with time along with Bess's fear and resentment. Getting ready for work one morning with the TV on Bess, found herself listening to the headlines of a woman that had been killed the night before by her husband. Bess's knees felt weak and a question ran through her mind. Is that the way it's going to be? Is that how my family is going to hear about my death?

Something happened inside Bess at that moment. She remembered the Teddy Bear and the knife through its back that she had found face down on the kitchen counter one morning. The blows, the doubt, and the forever feeling of fear. At that moment a decision was made, a plan of escape.

Bess had been thinking for some time on how to get away from Cole. Her life was in his hands and it was a very dangerous situation. She must be very careful not to alert him of anything.

Bess finally went to Cole and told him that she wanted to go back to school. She had always wanted to get into the field of architecture. The company was running strong and they had leased additional office space and hired additional personnel. Bess felt the company could run well without her presence and saw an opportunity to fulfill a dream of hers. Cole accepted this much better than she had anticipated. Bess enrolled in a local state college. Her plan was taking shape.

Chapter 12

"The Lord your God is with you, the mighty one will save you" (NCV)
Zephariah 3:17

It was coming up on Bess and Cole's fifth anniversary. As strange as it seemed, Bess wanted to do something special for Cole. Bess knew in her heart that her marriage to Cole would not last much longer. It couldn't, she thought, it's much too dangerous, but she still loved him. She loved his usually sweet nature, his kindness and his desire to help others. He was a good provider and earnestly wanted to do well. In spite of everything, Bess believed that everyone deserved a second chance many times over. She knew God had given her numerous second chances and she was no better than anyone else.

Bess decided on a new wedding band for Cole to replace the two he had thrown away, one out the truck window and one down the garbage disposal. The new band was embedded with five diamonds, one for each of the years they had been married.

Bess and Cole went back to Gatlinburg to celebrate. They were driving up to Clingman's Dome when Bess asked Cole to take the next pull off. Bess told Cole she had something for him. He pulled over and Bess handed him the wrapped box. "Happy anniversary honey," she said, and gave him a gentle kiss. Cole unwrapped the box and slowly opened it. Bess wasn't big on jewelry, but Cole loved giving it and thought this idea would work well for him.

"Oh sweetheart, wow, I love it!" Cole said. He sat for a long moment staring at it. He looked at Bess, his eyes filled with tears, "I really love it Bess and I'm so sorry for everything." Cole knew, and Bess too, that the two of them had not worked hard to make their marriage work. Cole knew he had cheated on Bess. He knew there were things he had done she knew nothing about. Bess felt a tug of hope in his eyes and the guilt ripped at her as she looked at him. She knew her plan was to get out. She looked back at him and took his hand. "Everything will be all right Cole, I love you," Bess assured him, as they drove on in silence.

Chapter 13

*"may the Lord watch over you
and give you peace" (NCV)*
Numbers 6:26

By this time Cole had decided they had out grown their small house. Bess loved the countryside and had been looking as well. They looked at land but didn't seem to be getting anywhere until a friend of Bess's showed her a piece of property with four acres and a some what rundown house. The land was perfect, four level acres that looked out at Whispering Pine Mountain. The house was set 500 yards back off the road. The front of the property was full of pines, azaleas, rhododendrons, and crepe myrtles. Three of the four acres were fenced and would be great for the dogs. There were muscadine grapevines in the back along with peach, apple and pear trees. One side of the property was shaded with huge oaks which made a wonderful place to walk.

As much as she loved the land, Bess thought the house needed too much work. Cole took over and convinced Bess it was the place they both longed for. She finally gave in and her heart and soul became this wonderful place. They remodeled inside and out and added a pool. It was done and Bess thought it could not be more perfect. Bess absolutely adored this place. They moved into the house in early August. Cole was scheduled to be on the road a lot and Bess was preparing for her final exam. Graduation was scheduled for the end of August.

For the first couple of weeks that Bess and Cole were in their new home there were many fights. Cole seemed to always come home around 7:30 to 8:00 in the evenings and had been drinking. Bess always had dinner ready whether he wanted to eat or not and usually he did not. These were very fragile times for Bess. She knew anything could set Cole off. She usually just offered him a glass of wine and hoped he would eventually fall asleep.

Chapter 14

"He who guards you never sleeps." (NCV)
Psalm 121:3

Bess answered the phone and heard her favorite uncle's voice on the other line. "Hey kiddo!"

"Hey Ross, how are you?"

"I'm afraid I have some bad news. It's John, he died of a heart attack last night."

Tears filled Bess's eyes as she listened to her uncle's explanation of the funeral arrangements. John was her mother's oldest brother and such a fun man to be around. Now he's with mom she assured herself. She told Ross she would see him tomorrow at the funeral.

Bess hung up and called Cole. "Hey Baby," Cole responded.

"Cole, my uncle John has died and I will be going to the funeral tomorrow, will you be going?" Bess secretly hoped he would not.

"No, Bess, you know I have to leave for California tomorrow."

"I know," Bess replied, "just checking."

The funeral was sad, but it was so good for Bess to be with her family. These were people that had loved her all her life. Here with them, she felt her back straighten and her head held higher. To them she represented so much more, a reflection of her mother. They knew nothing of the horrid life she existed in. They saw a woman of success and strength. They had no idea how much she needed them or how badly her heart ached as she had to leave them. On the long drive home she couldn't get them out of her mind.

When she arrived home the house was empty. Cole was supposed to have left that day on a long trip to the west coast. She looked forward to his absence. I'll just call the office real quick, she thought, just to be sure he had gotten away. Olan, one of Cole's employees, answered the phone and Bess's question worried him. "You mean he's not home yet? He should have been home long ago." Olan told Bess. "You better start calling the jails."

"Why?" Bess asked.

"He left here about an hour and half ago and he was wasted," Olan answered.

"I thought he would be on his way to California," Bess said flatly.

"Well he won't make it very far." Olan quipped.

"Great." was Bess's response and she hung up thinking I don't guess I should have expected anything less.

8:30 PM and Bess was pacing. The phone rang, it was Cole. "Where are you?" she asked.

"They picked me up for DUI; I need you to come get me." Cole sounded afraid and definitely not sober.

"I will not come get you." Bess responded, determined to stay within the boundaries she had set long ago.

"Bess, please come and get me, I need you."

"I will not Cole, I have told you 100 times I would not come and get you out of jail if you were picked up for DUI."

"Bess, please." but before he could say anything else Bess hung up.

Nervously, she thought about what she had just done. It was unforgivable, in Cole's eyes. She had betrayed him and abandoned him. Bess knew he would be furious. The phone rang, Bess answered, "Bess don't hang up. You have to come get me. I can't call anyone else, I need you." Bess hung up the phone without responding. What are you doing, she asked herself. You're reacting, not thinking. He'll kill you. This was deliberate refusal to help her husband. Twice he had said I need you.

The phone rang again; Bess picked it up and placed it back on the receiver. I thought you were only allowed one phone call from jail she thought. The phone rang several more times, she didn't answer. Bess paced the house going from room to room, making sure doors were locked and bolted and windows were shut and locked. She went downstairs and checked the garage and playroom and went outside and made sure the gate was shut. Cole wouldn't remember the code she assured herself. She brought the dogs and cats in with her upstairs and they huddled together as she tried to calm her head and arrange her thoughts. Her heart was pounding and she was scared for her life. Bess knew what kind of danger she was putting herself in.

Half knowingly, she pulled the phone book out and looked up Hunter County Sheriff's department. She found herself speaking to someone and telling them her story, the fact that her husband was in jail and she had refused to help, how dangerous he could be and how afraid she was. They asked her where he was, city or county, and Bess didn't know. They checked for her and found he was in city jail. They had picked him up around 8:00 that night. They would hold him for eight hours and then he would be released. "He can't come here," Bess could barely talk. She was feeling bad for him now, locked up in that awful place. How could she have done this to him? After all, he was her husband. Bess shook the thoughts from her head and listened to the voice on the other end of the line.

"Ma'am, I'm sorry, but we cannot stop him from coming home. Would you like for me to have the Domestic Task force call you?"

"Yes," Bess answered.

With her head back against the wall, Bess slowly lowered herself to the floor. It was well after midnight and sleep was unthinkable but suddenly she felt herself slipping. Candy, Bess and Cole's female cocker, crawled up into her lap and Bess hugged her close. Candy's so sensitive, Bess thought. Although all of them could read her moods and feel the tension she lived with, Candy was the most sensitive to it all. Bess became lost in those horrifying moments of rage and anger, thinking of the dogs hiding and trembling, and often having to clean up after Candy.

The phone rang and startled Bess. A strong but soothing voice was on the line. The caller introduced herself with the Domestic Violence Task Force. While calming Bess a little, she explained the procedures, what an order of protection was, how to obtain one and encouraged her to call the sheriff's department should she hear from Cole.

Bess thanked them for calling and hung up and looked at the clock, it was 2:00 AM. I've got to get some sleep she told herself and went and layed down, tossed for a while but finally fell asleep.

About 4:30 AM the phone rang, waking Bess, it was the sheriff's department. "We are releasing your husband."

Bess almost shouted into the phone, "You can't let him come here," she repeated for the second time that night.

"I'm sorry Mrs. Green, but there is nothing we can do. We cannot hold him any longer."

"Thank you," was all Bess could say.

Bess sat up in bed, thinking seemed hard. She just wanted to sleep, she was so tired and couldn't feel any where near the strength that she knew she needed to face this day. She layed back, drifted off to sleep. The phone rang again. It was Cole. "Bess, I'll be home in about an hour."

"Okay," replied Bess.

The door bell rang. Oh my God Bess thought. She peeked out the front window to see two police cars in her driveway. She rushed to the front door and slung it open. The storm door was latched and she couldn't get the lock undone, she was shaking so badly. Finally, speaking through the door she said "I can't get it open, can you meet me down stairs?" She met the two policemen outside in the carport. "How did you get in here?' she asked them, worried. "I had the gate closed and locked, how did you get in here?"

"The gate was wide open ma'am."

"Open," Bess repeated. She distinctly remembered making sure the gate was closed and locked the night before. She checked and rechecked through the night. She was remembering the night and the measures she had taken to make sure she was safe and secure.

"You've heard from your husband?" The policeman said, getting her attention.

"Yes," she answered," he should be here soon." The officers could tell she was frantic with fear.

"You don't have to live like this," they told her. "The beatings will not stop, no matter what he tells you, no matter what you choose to believe." Bess knew this time they were right.

Another police car pulled up to the house and the patrolman asked where the husband was as he got out of his patrol car. They were standing in the carport when they heard the truck coming up the driveway. "Is that your husband?"

"Yes," said Bess.

Cole jumped out of the truck, disheveled and shoe strings missing from his tennis shoes. He stomped toward Bess and the policemen. "You didn't have to call out the blasted military Bess," he snapped. Bess shook with fear. Cole started into the house.

"You don't have any weapons in the house do you?" they asked Cole.

He responded "I don't, she might," pointing to Bess. Bess started in the house behind Cole, fearful he would try to take Archie with him. They stopped her.

"Just stay here with us," they said. They allowed Cole to go in and get a change of clothes.

Bess could sense their fear. Of course they are afraid, she thought, they have no idea what he is capable of. Cole returned with an armload of clothes. What Bess didn't know was that he had taken all the cash that was in the house. Cole was allowed to leave, and was asked not to return.

The police asked her what her plans were, and she told them that she would be divorcing Cole, feeling as if someone else were speaking for her. They urged her to get an Order of Protection and to call 911 immediately if Cole gave her any trouble. She thanked them over and over and walked down and closed the gate as they left.

Bess came back into the house, and although it was August she opened up the hall closet and pulled a throw around her shoulders and went and sat at her desk which overlooked her beautiful front yard, but her eyes could only see that gate. I know, I know, I checked that gate over and over last night. I am the only one with the code at the gate and the only one with a remote here at the house that will open that gate. Bess lingered with that thought for quite some time. God opened that gate. It's the only logical explanation. God opened that gate. Had that gate been closed and locked those policemen likely would have turned and left. They would not have climbed that gate and walked unprotected to this house. God opened that gate. Bess put her face in her hands and just listened to her heart beating and thanked God for saving her life that day.

The first call Bess made was to an attorney. She left a message illustrating her situation and an hour or so later the attorney returned her call. Bess was instructed to go to the courthouse to the fourth floor and ask for Heather. Heather did all the paperwork and took her down to the second floor to appear before a judge who granted an order of protection. She was instructed to keep the order with her at all times. The police would need to see it if she had a reason to use it. If Cole as much as even hinted at harming her, he would be picked up and put in jail. Bess knew that would not stop Cole, but it was the only peace of mind she had.

The days that followed for Bess were trying and terrifying. Cole had taken all the money that was in the house. He had sent one of his employees to pick up the vehicle Bess had as he said he needed it for the business, and she had no income. Bess practically boarded herself inside the house with the cats and dogs. But, she knew in her heart that there would be restitution. Looking out her front window she saw nothing but beauty, and out the back door, Whispering Pine Mountain. These free gifts form God brought Bess much comfort. He will take care of me, Bess told herself over and over. He will take care of me.

Chapter 15

"The sufferings we have now are nothing compared to the great glory that will be shown to us." (NCV)
Romans 8:18

Bess had been all over the internet and through the papers. She must have sent out 100 resumes. But nothing was coming in. She picked up the phone and called the warehouse for Cole and asked to speak to him. "Hey baby," he said, Bess gritted her teeth.

"Cole, I have no money, the water, phone, and electric companies are threatening to cut off service. Will you please send some money? The bills are still your responsibility."

"I don't have any money to send you Bess. Business is slow; you know it slows down this time of year. Maybe you should have thought twice before you kicked me out. Guess you're just going to have to get a job."

"Cole, I am trying to get a job. I've sent out 100 resumes. But even if I did have a job, I couldn't get to it." Bess tried to keep her composure, but she wanted to scream.

"Sorry," Cole answered, "I'm really sorry Bess," and hung up.

I hate him, Bess thought, and then realized for the first time she did hate him. She felt sick and wanted to lie down and just give up.

Again, as she had done a dozen times before, she searched through drawers. Cole would hide money anywhere. She knew there had been $900 in Cole's sock drawer the night before he was picked up for DUI. Why had she not hidden it herself? Probably better that she hadn't she thought, just something else to set him off. Bess found nothing. She went to her closet and reached for the cup. It was full of silver dollars and Susan B Anthony's, $45. She should just take it she thought. It was part of Cole's collection. It's not mine, Bess told herself, and put it back.

Bess and Cole had been running a business for six years and suddenly Bess was without income or a job. She ran through the classifieds and applied at a local temp service. She ran across a part-time job for an insurance agency, which she had insisted she would never get back into but applied there also. She had to have an income. She was hired as a receptionist at a local car dealership and went to interview at the insurance agency. One thing Bess had in her favor was the court ordered Cole to provide her with a vehicle. She was welcomed in and waited on a couch for the interviewer to ask her in. Bess was ready to bolt. Do I really want to get back into this rat race again, she asked herself. Something kept her there for several minutes as she argued with herself. Something kept her there.

She was interviewed and offered the job. It would pay $8 an hour and the receptionist job at the car dealership would pay $9 an hour. She took both jobs. It was income she told herself, she had to eat and feed her family of four leggers. She also found a sub-contract job for an architect in Georgia that would be a little money too.

The money she was making didn't come near the enormous bills she had. Her only option was her credit cards. She paid her biggest bills with credit cards. It never entered her mind the debt she was building because she was in survival mode. But Bess also wanted a life of something more than just making ends meet. She wanted to live.

Chapter 16

*"He takes care of his people like a shepherd.
He gathers them like lambs in his arms
and carries them close to him." (NCV)*
Isaiah 40:11

Bess had become good friends with a couple of girls at the insurance agency. Diane approached Bess one day at work. "Hey Bess," Laura, my daughter's, sixteenth birthday is Saturday the first, just a few weeks away. Laura is hoping to have a party at your place, what do you think?" Bess was thrilled.

"Of course, it's perfect!" Bess knew with all the room and the pool it would be a great place to have a teenage birthday party.

She bought dozens of colorful balloons and lined the driveway and deck with them. She decorated the house with them along with many of her stuffed teddy bears. She also had a friend in town who was celebrating his birthday as well. He came in a day early and helped Bess get the place ready, mowing and cleaning. The next day she got balloons, bears, cake, drinks and utensils ready. People started to arrive and presents were piled high on the kitchen table. It was early October and a bit chilly. The kids tried to swim but it was too cool. They chatted and Laura opened gifts while they had cake. Just before everyone started to leave, Bess and Diane gathered up balloons and gave each kid a bundle. They went out to the back of Bess's property and turned them all loose. It was a beautiful sight, seeing all those colors against the bright blue October sky. Diane let out a big sigh, "There goes Laura's youth!" Bess laughed out loud and hugged her friend.

Over and over and over, again Bess went to court fighting for a divorce from Cole. Every two weeks and nothing was moving forward. The judge would order Cole to bring evidence of the company's financials to court and every two weeks he showed up with nothing. Finally Cole agreed to take on the business bills and debt and the second mortgage on the house while Bess agreed to the rest of the personal bills and debt.

Bess was visiting a friend in Foxwoods, Tennessee and got a call from the bank that held the second mortgage, Cole had not been making the payments.

The loan was three months behind and the bank was threatening foreclosure. Bess was furious, finally furious. She told the banker that foreclosure was not going to happen. They had a heated argument. She hung up the phone and called the president of the bank, whom she knew, and flatly told him to have the banks attorney call her attorney and the two of them could settle this. Bess received a call a day or two later from the bank saying they were backing off the foreclosure.

As hard as Bess tried she just could not make ends meet and she was running out of credit and time. She came home from work on a Friday night and was too weary to think. She poured herself some vodka and sat down, her head whirling, but her mind beginning to relax. She lifted the glass, looked at it, and said out loud, "You are my only friend."

She thought of all that had happened to her. It had all happened so fast. About her escape and new hope, which seemed to be fading. She remembered one day listening to a local Christian radio station and the testimony of the owner and she had pulled over and wept and asked Jesus again to rescue her. She thought of her options. I'm out of money, I can't pay the bills, they are threatening to take my home, what will I do with the kids; everything was swirling and swirling in Bess's mind as she poured another drink.

Bess was defeated. She had no energy or reason to go on. She got dressed for bed and went to the bathroom to brush her teeth; still very down she looked for a bottle of pills. She pulled out a bottle of muscle relaxers that she had as a treatment for a neck injury. Bess thought, I could end this now, all I want to do is sleep, and not wake up.

Bess emptied the bottle into her hand. She counted the pills… thirteen. This she thought will bring me peace. Shaking, she looked again, and counted again.

She put them back in the bottle and put them back in the cabinet.

She went to bed sobbing.

Bess thought to herself, I'm going to smother myself to death. Stop it! Her nails dug deep into the pillow she had wrapped around her head, her sobs were coming hard and she could hardly catch her breath. She remembered the night before and the chance she took. The choice she almost made and how God pulled her back. Although she put the bottle of pills away she was still frightened of herself right now. Could she face herself, her weakness? The sobs were harder than even the night before. She knew she had chosen to live, and that choice in itself seemed to offer so little. It was a battle she felt she was not prepared to fight. "I can't do this," she sobbed.

The Glory of Hope

Sun flickered through the curtains and warmed her face and Bess could feel a bit of life again. All she wanted to do was sleep, but she turned and stretched and slowly pulled herself upright. She found herself looking eye to eye with a picture of Jesus holding a lamb. She stared hard at it. Huge tears started down her checks again. Where are you? It was as if she wanted to argue with someone. As far as she was concerned her life was over. But there He was, looking back at her. Those eyes seemed to speak to her. And the lamb He was holding… it was her, it's me isn't it Bess thought. I am the Lamb, aren't I? And, you are with me, aren't you? She heard a voice strong and stern in her heart. "Yes."

She kept staring back at the picture and as she did it was as if something were being born. At first she didn't want to see it, she didn't want to feel it, but she couldn't move. For the first time in so many years hope was knocking at her door. She was so afraid and uncertain that she fought with herself to believe that there was such a thing. She stared and the picture stared back. Finally she flung the covers off of her. Barriers she thought; I have surrounded myself with barriers. I am the one who is limiting myself. The world is open to me and I can't be afraid, or I will die, die from fear. She almost ran to the shower.

She had the water warmer than usual but Bess could feel she was being cleansed, cleansed from the dragons of the past. She felt the power of the water on her face and down her back. She reveled in it. My life, it is beginning again. This time the tears were not of sorrow or doubt, but of hope and faith and Bess stood there still and let the water take over her doubts.

Bess dressed and went for a long run. Her headset playing the song rang to her… "am I to blame for what I'm not or is pain the way God teaches me to grow? I need to know. Does the thorn become a blessing, or does the pain become a friend. When does the weakness make me stronger, when does my faith make me whole again? I want to feel His arms around me in the middle of my raging storm, so that I can see the blessing in the storm."

Jogging back home was sweet, Bess felt stronger than she had in such a long time. She dove into the pool and stayed there for quite some time. She was alone and looking out over her back yard and up at Whispering Pine Mountain. Bess felt powerful and at the same time peaceful. She pulled herself out of the pool and headed into the house. She was tired from the roller coaster of emotions. She showered again and stretched out on the couch. She snuggled with Candy and Archie and fell fast asleep in the middle of the day.

The Glory of Hope

Bess knew she had to let go. She knew her life depended on it. What she didn't know was that her soul had to be resurrected, because that part of her had died. She had no idea what a struggle she had before her. But, she had begun.

Chapter 17

*"You are my place of safety and protection.
You are my God and I trust you." (NCV)*
Psalm 91:2

Bess started picking plums from a tree that she was told was ornamental. Well, Bess thought otherwise. She picked, cleaned, cut, boiled and made a great plum jelly! She loved the place she lived, full of tall oaks, fruit trees and flowering bushes. She looked out the back at Whispering Pine Mountain and watched it change with the seasons which always gave her great hope. She often would be visited by skunks and soaring eagles. Bess learned so much the two years she spent there. She learned so much about herself, her own soul, and the souls of others and how sacred that was. Her relationship with God grew and grew and she was so very thankful for every single day, even though she was still battling to divorce Cole.

She enjoyed her neighbor, Mrs. Harris. She was retired and had moved to the small farm next door less than two years before Bess moved in. It was to be her and her husband's retirement place. However, her husband was diagnosed with cancer not long after and had passed away before Bess arrived. Mrs. Harris was a hardworking lady. She had cattle that she tended to, and a huge vegetable garden that she plowed and sowed herself. Bess would get together with her and her family on occasion. They would play guitars and sing. They were quite talented and Bess enjoyed being with them.

Bess was in the back of her property picking grapes, when on the other side something pulled. It pulled again and again. Bess walked around to see Archie pulling grapes from the vine. Bess laughed and hugged him. "Helping mom out?" she asked him. She looked at the mountain and the sky and thanked God endlessly.

Sometimes, Bess told herself, you have to give yourself time for peace to enter and stay. And she did. Bess chose to stay close to her home and her little family. It was so safe there and it had become a refuge for her. Just to come home and feel peace and feel safe. She loved it so much. Just looking out a window and not worrying about the end of the day. Peace was so sacred.

Bess hung up the phone from a long conversation with a friend. It was storming, and the minute she put the phone back in the base a huge bolt of lightening jolted her and the house. She practically fell to the floor. What was that her mind raced? She was quiet but could hear a sound, it sounded like a cow mooing she thought. Then from the crouched position she was in she looked up and there on the refrigerator was the cow magnet she had and yes it was mooing. The bolt of lightning that hit her house with such force caused the mooing magnet to go off! Bess, started to laugh. That's crazy she thought. Then she smelled smoke. Oh my gosh! Bess picked the phone up but it was dead. She reached for her cell and called 911.

It only took a few minutes before the firemen arrived. They went through her entire house and into the attic. There was only damage to a spot near the corner of the house where the lightening had struck that had caused a very slight burn. Everything electronic had been knocked out, including the security system and gate. Bess thanked the firemen who assured her everything looked okay, but said to call if she smelled smoke again. The insurance company covered all the damage less her deductible, and had everything replaced and repaired within a couple of weeks. It was drama, but drama Bess could handle at this point.

The job at the insurance agency began to really work for Bess even though she had said she would never get back into insurance. God had pushed her back and Bess had returned reluctantly. But it really was the best thing that had happened to her. The owners were very good to her and gave her a chance to grow. She soon made the decision to ask if she could have a fulltime job and let go of her job at the car dealership. Bess knew she needed to support herself with the skill that she had and that was her knowledge of insurance. She wanted to move into a marketing position with the agency and discussed it with one of the owners. She was met with resistance but he gave her a shot at it and it paid off. She came into her office one Monday morning and her boss had put a post it note on her desk that read "You can move into the marketing office, the job is yours!" Bess was elated! She enjoyed the position and everyone was so gracious to her. Bess found it hard at first to cozy up to anyone, but eventually she did and formed some great lifetime friends at the agency.

Bess, AJ and Diane, friends form the agency, lounged around the pool having a few drinks and munching on just about anything they could get their hands on. They laughed until they were doubled over, had an early dinner and went down stairs to watch a movie. AJ fell asleep early and Diane and Bess stayed up and watched City of Angels and cried. It was a great girl's day and night.

AJ was taking a sales training course in Florida that took her there four times a year. Bess joined her for a couple of trips. The classes were in Ft Lauderdale and Bess and AJ met up on Sanibel Island. AJ had gotten them a hotel room. Bess knocked on the door and AJ answered. The two girls hugged and jumped up and down with delight in the hallway squealing like two teenagers! Another guest was coming up the steps and Bess and AJ, embarrassed, jumped back into the hotel room. AJ was so excited about her class and started telling Bess all about it. They sat down in the floor with a glass of wine each, with shrimp cocktail and Doritos and talked until late into the night. The next morning they set out to explore the island. It was a small place and not very commercial. They rode up to the end of the adjoining island, which is known as Captiva, and had a delicious lunch at a small café out on the porch overlooking the bay.

They spent hours walking around visiting shops and riding bikes on trails. They had the best ice cream they both said that they had ever had. They took a water taxi over to Cabbage Key and had burgers made famous by Jimmy Buffet. There were a momma dolphin and two babies that joined them on the trip swimming in the wake of the boat. It was a beautiful, warm and sunny day, and Bess and AJ had a blast.

On the plane on the trip back both girls were pretty quiet. They had such a great time and didn't seem to have a care in the world for a few days. They were both a little homesick already for the serenity of the island.

Pulling up to the gate Bess smiled. She had a great time in Florida, but she was glad to be home. Candy and Homer were at the gate, all wags, to greet her. Bess rolled down the window, "Where's Archie?" Bess asked her pups. She pushed the remote to open the gate and pulled slowly up to the house as Candy and Homer danced around her truck, but still no sign of Archie. Bess pulled in the carport and hopped out and was greeted again by Candy and Homer jumping and wagging. She stepped out of the carport and called for Archie a few times.

She heard the flap on the doggie door snap shut and turned to see Archie standing there looking very weak with his head lowered almost touching the floor. Bess hurried to him. She saw blood but couldn't tell really much else. She raised the garage door and took him inside where she could examine him further. What she saw turned her stomach. Archie's flesh was torn almost all the way around one of his front

The Glory of Hope

legs. She saw raw muscle and tissue to the bone. The bleeding had, however, stopped.

Bess was outraged. Mrs. Harris, who watched her dogs while she was away, was on her mower. Bess's anger was almost out of control. She didn't even think about the kindness of her neighbor for caring for her kids, as Bess often referred to her pets. She was furious. She ran over to where her neighbor was mowing and took her by the arm to get her attention. "Mrs. Harris, shut the engine off," Bess demanded. "What happened to Archie?" Bess was almost screaming at her.

"I don't know what you're talking about Bess."

"He's hurt bad," Bess replied. The two ran back to Archie. Mrs. Harris took a look at Archie and could not believe what she saw.

"Oh my goodness, Bess." Mrs. Harris helped her get Archie into a kennel and into the truck. Bess raced to the animal emergency hospital forty-five minutes away.

Archie was examined. Bess was told it could be an hour or more before they could get him cleaned up and stitched up. He was very lucky. There did not appear to be any nerve damage, and he should heal just fine.

Bess was not far from a local hang out she would go to and meet up with friends. She was harried by the whole ordeal and the long trip home and was hungry. She walked in and a few friends were there. She ordered a drink and something to eat and told them about her trip and about what had happened to Archie. They poked fun at her for being there while her son "was in surgery". She was glad to have them as friends. They knew how much she loved her kids and making light of things helped calm her.

Later, after discussing the events of that day, Mrs. Harris and Bess concluded that Archie and one, or both of her dogs, had gotten ahold of him through the fence and torn him up pretty badly. Mrs. Harris found a tooth belonging to one of her dogs on her side of the fence. They were both pretty shaken from the ordeal and Mrs. Harris felt badly. Both were very thankful that Archie was going to be okay.

Chapter 18

*"I will make you wise and show you where to go.
I will guide you and watch over you." (NCV)*
Psalm 32:8

Bess loved the home she and Cole had, although Cole was only there for a couple of weeks prior to the separation. Bess spent many hours just mowing the four acres. She found so much peace and strength in mowing. Her headset blaring and her singing along at the top of her lungs, Bess admired the mountain behind the house and the setting sun. Nothing could be better for her right now as far as she was concerned. She had withdrawn herself from others during her marriage to Cole and now she was secluding herself inside the peace and her own space that she found in her home. She was learning who she was again and her purpose in life. At one time giving up seemed her only option, but now she could feel herself growing within. She was beginning to smile a lot to herself and understand her own emotions, even if no one else did. What mattered to Bess now was that she knew she didn't need acceptance from anyone else, just from herself. The road was long and rough, Bess could see it before her and she knew it was her only option. Take it and make it.

She took a quick shower and put on her favorite bathing suit and set up her spot on the deck by the pool. She put her favorite CD in the player and lay back. What a perfect day. She picked up the book she had been reading. The few sessions with a counselor had helped her so much to realize her own value, to realize this was her life and hers to live.

But Bess still felt something was missing. Like an itch she could not reach. Something was lacking and she just couldn't put her finger on it. "That's it," Bess sighed; the book she was reading had suggested something. "That's it!" Bess put the book aside and gazed at the clear blue sky. "To give back," she whispered.

A few days later Bess pulled in the drive and hopped out of her pickup truck to get the mail. She immediately heard the bright crisp song of a bird. Bess stopped and looked around. Just above her on the power line was a mockingbird singing its heart out. Bess walked on to the mailbox and started back to the truck. The bird was still singing away. Bess stopped and listened for several minutes. She felt there was a message in the songs of that bird. She felt the presence of her mother and grandmother, and Patch, whom she had just recently buried. Bess smiled and thought the mockingbird represented the females she had lost in her life and the song brightness for her future. Bess had a new guardian angel! She smiled, said a quick thank you to God and slowly pulled her truck in the carport.

That same week Bess was getting out of her truck at work when she heard those same familiar songs. She stepped out of her truck and saw a mockingbird just a few feet away sitting on a railing. Bess was surprised and just stood for a moment and watched and listened. She thought to name the bird, Hestia, Goddess of hearth and home. What a great way to start a day she thought.

Bess had been working at a local Family and Children's Service with other women who had been involved in the same type relationship that she had experienced. It was an emotionally trying job. But Bess knew she needed to help. She had done a local TV spot on domestic violence and was working on putting together a Public Service Announcement. Writing helped her tremendously.

Working on the PSA was a huge task. She had found a song that she thought worked beautifully with what she had in mind. The artist lived in Nashville and the publisher was Sony in California. It took quite a bit of doing, but she finally received the authorization from both to use the song and was granted limited time of air space. A friend of hers put the piece together on a cassette. But to Bess it still wasn't enough and she had this nagging sense of lack of accomplishment. At the same time she was somewhat reluctant to make public what she knew so privately, especially in the same place where Cole and she had their business. Bess weighed her options. Maybe I need to make a fresh start, she thought.

As much as Bess loved her home and the beauty it held right outside her doors she knew she could not hold onto it much longer. The salary she was making fell quite short of the income she needed to support it all and she knew her debt would only continue to mount, trying to keep up and enjoying it all in the meantime.

She sat on the deck looking out at Whispering Pine Mountain and the massive oak trees that lined the property between her and her neighbor. Bess felt she would not have made it through the past twenty two months without the peace and serenity this place had brought her. Yes, there were constant struggles making ends meet but all in all it had brought her great strength and comfort. Bess watched as Archie, Candy and Homer sniffed things out in the far back of her property. They too loved the freedom and space of this place. Bess could see the horses grazing on the small farm behind her and could hear the geese coming in to light on Mrs. Harris's pond. She closed her eyes and let the sweet natural sound of life surround her.

It had taken twenty two months but Bess and Cole's divorce had been finalized. She kicked around the thought of moving back to her home town. She wanted to be closer to her family and friends from school.

Bess put together her resume and mailed it out to about six insurance agencies she was familiar with in the Nashville area. She quickly had a response from a fairly large agency and an interview was scheduled for a Saturday. Bess made the drive up and met for a couple of hours with the agency's primary owner and office manager. The position was for Assistant Marketing Manager. The appointment went well and Bess loved the office and area where it was located. After more discussions with the agency an offer was made with a nice salary increase that Bess thought was necessary to make the move. She accepted the offer but dreaded the discussion she would have to have with her current employer. They had been so good to her and she had formed some lifetime friendships.

Bess sat down with her bosses and told them about the decision she had made. At first they didn't understand but once she explained her need to get back to her hometown, they were supportive and wished her well.

It didn't take long for the house to sell and Bess was making arrangements for a mover. She got a couple of estimates but the best was from a smaller moving company. Moving day came and there was some packing left to do for the movers. One of the movers recognized Cole in a photo. He told Bess that he knew him and that he currently worked for their company. Bess panicked and called the franchise owner and expressed concern. "Please sir," Bess pleaded, "Cole cannot know where I am going." The owner assured her this move would be confidential.

Chapter 19

"The God of all grace, who called you to His eternal glory in Christ after you have suffered a while, will himself restore you and make you strong, firm, and steadfast." (NCV)
1 Peter 5:10

Bess loaded her pickup truck with the essentials for the night ahead of her, a cot, sheets, and food. Bess gave the cats a slight sedative for their travel. She put them in small carriers and tied them down securely in the bed of the pickup truck. She wedged Archie, Candy and Homer into the cab of the truck. She had a three-hour drive ahead of her. Bess felt good about her future. She drove beyond the gate got out and locked it up. She looked back with tears streaming down her face. She loved this place, it had helped save her. It had given new strength to her soul. But Bess knew she had to keep moving.

She closed the gate and hopped in the cab of the truck with Archie, Candy and Homer and drove. She sang to herself most of the way. They were getting close to their new home when Homer became restless. Bess kept talking to him and trying to soothe his anxieties. They had been traveling almost three hours. Homer couldn't hold it any longer. He pooped in the floorboard. Bess rolled down her window and pinched her nose for the rest of the way.

When they arrived, Bess got the dogs out and cleaned up Homer's mess. She let the dogs out into the back yard, fixed the cats kitty litter, and made herself a sandwich. She then put sheets on the cot, got a pillow, and the six of them piled in. The moving truck would be there tomorrow and Bess slowly fell into a deep sleep.

Bess woke early and felt newness about her. A new beginning she thought. She let the dogs out and they ran and relaxed a little. The cats were locked up in the bathroom. Bess would not let them out of the house for a couple of weeks.

The movers arrived with Bess's furniture. The house was very small so things were cramped, but what Bess loved so much about the place was the space around it. It was on a busy highway but still there was a sense of peace, something that Bess had learned to love. Bess could look out the front door and

The Glory of Hope

see cattle grazing. The back yard was fenced and was a good run for the dogs.

After the furniture was unloaded, Bess drove to the grocery store. She ordered pizza for the night and watched her dogs romp and bark. She was exhausted and she was starting a new job on Monday. She poured herself a glass of wine and sat on the deck and looked out at the country before her. It was a new beginning and she was weary. She was afraid of failing. God had been so good to her.

Bess often threw a tennis ball against the house for the dogs to chase. She met the back yard neighbors, who were a nice couple with teenage children and a toddler grandchild. They were friendly with each other and often met at the fence for neighborly conversation. They watched over the dogs and cats for Bess if she had to be away or gone overnight. Her landlord was a deputy for the county sheriff's department and he would stop in from time to time and check on her.

Bess left for her first day at her new job. She was nervous, anxious, and excited all at the same time. It was a fifty minute drive one way. Bess didn't mind that at all. It was a highway through countryside most of the way until she got into the city. Traffic moved along at a steady pace.

When she arrived at the office she was met by the office manager, and they took care of the necessary paperwork for taxes and benefits enrollment. She took Bess around and introduced her to the employees she would be working with in her department. Everyone was welcoming and said they were excited to have her on board. Within the first three weeks of her employment she was moved from Assistant Marketing Manager to Marketing Manager. Things were moving very fast. Bess was elated, but also quite overwhelmed.

She enjoyed going to the more populated areas on the weekends, about a thirty minute drive from the rental house. She would do some casual shopping and stop for lunch at one of her favorite restaurants. She would linger for some time and spend much of that time writing. As tough as it was at times, she wrote mostly about her days with Cole, both the good and the bad.

Bess walked in the door of the house one Saturday after returning from shopping and lunch and put her things away. She had been running all day and was ready to wind down for the evening. She noticed the message light blinking on her answering machine and punched the button. "Bess, this is Cole, I need to talk to you. Please call me Monday." Bess did not recognize the voice or the name at first. She listened to the message over and over until finally she recognized it to be Cole.

"What does he want?" Bess said angrily. "How did he find me?"

Out of fear she quickly called the phone company. Trying to calm herself Bess said in a frantic voice, "I need to change my phone number and I need to have it unlisted." After a few minutes Bess hung up the phone with her new number, asking herself again, how did he find me and why, thinking back to the conversation she had with the owner of the moving company.

AJ and her husband, Camden, were visiting Bess. They had finished a late dinner and Camden watched a basketball game while AJ and Bess lounged in the living room watching a movie. When they got up to go to bed, Bess turned out the lights and they headed down the hallway when suddenly Bess collapsed. She came to slowly, hearing AJ's frantic voice, "Camden please do something!"

Bess rose to a sitting position, "What happened?" she asked weakly. Camden accused her of falling asleep. She looked at him in amazement and disbelief, "While I was walking?" she asked.

"Are you okay?" AJ asked.

"I think so," responded Bess, "I'm going to bed." She lay down but was quite shaky and concerned about what had just happened.

She rose early the next morning, but still was not feeling quite herself. It was a bright beautiful morning and she went out to let the dogs out of the garage. Sitting on the roof above the door to the garage was a mockingbird singing those familiar songs that she loved to hear. As she always did when she heard those songs she thought of all the strong females that were once in her life. She let out a sigh and thought to herself, everything's going to be all right.

Bess continued to have spells and found herself picking herself up off the floor while home alone. She once fainted and took a pretty good blow to the head when she fell. The next morning she called her doctor and made an appointment. Bess had heart issues since she was a young girl. The doctor detected a murmur and referred her to a cardiologist who put her through several tests. One was a tilt table test.

The doctor and nurse strapped Bess to a table flat on her back. They hooked her up to an EKG, blood pressure monitor and pulse rate monitor. They were watching her heart rate on a screen. They gradually began to tilt the table to a standing position, stopping at intervals and checking her vitals. When they started to get her to an upright position they gave Bess nitroglycerin. Bess started feeling faint and complained to the nurse that she wasn't feeling well. The next thing she knew she heard the nurse saying, "Ms. Clay? Ms. Clay? Open your eyes." Bess opened her eyes and she was back in the reclined position. "Looks like you passed the test," the nurse said smiling. Bess saw no humor in it. What she learned was that her heart rate was jumping seriously high then plummeting dangerously low. That is what was causing her fainting. The doctor put her on a medication to help regulate her heart rate. She was off of work for two weeks recuperating and so grateful she had an understanding employer.

Chapter 20

Year 2000

"But thanks be to God, who in Christ always leads us in triumphal procession and through us spreads, the fragrance of the knowledge of Him everywhere." (ESV)
2 Corinthians 2:14

Bess had been introduced to Donna who coordinated the local shelter for women escaping from domestic violence. She became involved with the group and was asked to give speeches to schools and other organizations. She volunteered to do so, much against the doubts that clouded her mind. But she took the challenge and took the step.

When Bess joined Donna at the Andrew Jackson Hotel, she was nervous and quiet; the doubts were back. Are you kidding yourself Bess? You really think that you can get up in front of all these people and say a single word, much less an entire speech, condensing the last few years in a few paragraphs? Why did you agree to this, what were you thinking? Donna had told her they were expecting about 300 people.

People mingled in and took their seats. Bess sat at a front table on a platform with Donna and other guests. Donna introduced everyone including Bess as the guest speaker. Bess was in a simple black dress that buttoned down the front and cap sleeves. I suddenly feel frumpy, Bess thought.

When it was time for Bess to speak, she drew a breath and walked forward. The crowd was much larger than she had imagined. She was trembling. But this was nothing. *She felt the cold hard blow of a fist against her face.* Memories swept up and enveloped her. She knew this was not about her, but about others. It was for others who may be facing the same things. She knew this was happening too many around her.

She stood and went to the podium and stared out at the sea of people. She placed her index cards with her speech in front of her, dropped her hands so that no one could see her uncontrollable shaking, and began; her voice, near a whisper.

The Glory of Hope

"Hi,

It's great to be back in Nashville. I had a wonderful childhood growing up here with my two brothers. I may have gone to school with some of you. We grew up in what I consider South Nashville and attended local public schools. I spent most of my twenties in West Nashville. Single and having a blast, not too serious about much of anything. In my late twenties, I met a man and followed him to Charleston. We eventually married, it didn't work out and we divorced. About a year and a half later, I met the man of my dreams. He was charming, loving, protective, strong, fun and he adored me. My life couldn't have been better.

Every 4 seconds a woman is being beaten

Do you know what it's like to be beaten? Some of you probably do.

I don't mean beaten at a sport, a game or a bet.

I mean pulling yourself off the floor, crawling to a nearby bed or chair, wondering how bad am I hurt? And waiting, barely breathing, so as not to be heard. Waiting for dawn and as it arrives, pulling yourself up and making your way to the bathroom to face your reflection. You're alive, reminding yourself, but I wish I wasn't another voice says.

> *As Bess is speaking memories start to creep in from a dark corner of her life... she darts from Cole into the bathroom and shuts and locks the door. Cole is shouting at her from the other side of the door. Bess looks up... the window... Bess races and raises the window, knocks out the screen, hauls herself up... and jumps...*

We cling to hope that it will end

I wanted my marriage to work. I loved my husband. I didn't want to fail, not again. I made a promise, a vow to my husband and to God, a lifetime vow. I couldn't break that vow. That was against everything that I believed in, if it would just stop. I could live with the rest. This didn't happen in other homes, I was sure of that, why only mine? I just wanted to be happy like all the others. We could be so happy, only if. He needed me, he really needed me. If I could just find a way to fix it.

> *Bess recalls the feel of her face being slammed into her desk, her face catching the stapler, the*

cut lip and the black eye. How dazed she was and how quick it all had happened, and why? What did I do?

Each day 4 women are killed by a domestic violence situation

One morning I got out of bed and went to the kitchen for a glass of water. There in the kitchen was one of my collections of Teddy Bears. It was face down on the countertop with a butcher knife stabbed down through its back. I stopped and gasped. There was a note scribbled with something about "everyone stabbing him in the back."

I was trembling, what did this mean? What had happened? We didn't argue last night. Mornings were usually our better time of the days. What was going through his mind, what lied ahead for me? I didn't dare bring it up though. I didn't dare mention it.

Bess stares at the bear, facedown, the knife plunged into its back. She tugs at the knife; its force has it stuck in the counter top. She tugs again and it comes out and she pulls it out of the back of the teddy bear. There is a deep gouge in the counter top. She's trembling…

Jo Barron Hardy

30% of deaths to women are due to homicide

I was getting ready to go to work one morning and had the local news on as usual and there was a story of a woman who had been killed the night before by her husband during an argument. Was that the way it was going to be? Was that the way my family and friends would hear about my death?

Bess raises her head, the room is black. Where am I? She tries to shake the cobwebs. She remembers the fists, the kicking, how she was trying to protect herself, curled in a ball. She quietly pulls herself from the floor to the bed without standing or making a sound. She covers herself and waits in black silence.

After eight years of marriage, it ended. My husband was picked up for DUI and put in jail. He called for me to come and get him. I told him I would not. He continued to call; I would not talk to him. I knew he was furious, more than ever. I called the sheriff's department and explained the situation. The domestic task force was on the phone with me through the night. I knew this was it. I was scared to death, but I knew this was my only chance. He was so furious with me if he ever got near me he would kill me.

It wouldn't have stopped this time, until it was too late. The police informed me when they released him from jail and he called me to tell me he was on his way home. There were three policemen at our home when he arrived. As I anticipated he was furious; the police could tell, he spouted something to me about having called out the military, almost mocking the police. Daring them. The police asked him if he had a weapon in the house, and they let him go inside to get a change of clothes. I know they were as frightened as I was. They told me I didn't have to live like this, that he could kill me, and the beatings would continue as long as I stayed, no matter what I thought. This time though, I believed them, this time I knew they were telling the truth.

Bess's mind drifts again... to that night, looking out the windows and doors making sure the gate was closed and locked. She knew she was the only one that had the code to open that gate. But, when the police arrived, how had they gotten to the house? She insisted to them that the gate was closed and locked and she was the only one with the code. The police insisted it was "wide open." God! The policemen would not have come to the house if that gate had not been opened, Bess knew that. God opened that gate that morning. God saved her life.

Later that morning, I called an attorney, that afternoon I was in court filling for an Order of Protection.

I was afraid, very afraid. The risk of death is 70% greater during the initial separation. I would not leave the house, for ten days I stayed locked up inside. I was afraid he would burn the house down. I felt safer there than on the outside.

I was just finishing school when we separated. I had no money and no way to pay the bills that supported our somewhat lavish lifestyle. The utilities were going to be cut off; the house payments weren't being made. I was going to lose my home. Everything was mounting. I couldn't hold it off. I didn't have the strength to fight this. The past was calling. Was I going to have to give in?

I dumped a bottle of pills in my hand, thirteen to be exact; muscle relaxers. Those pills represented peace, in an overwhelming way. What were my choices, giving in or giving up? Giving up seemed the better option. I would rather die than go back. It was the loneliest place I had ever been. I don't know what prompted me, but I put the pills back in the bottle and

The Glory of Hope

went to bed and sobbed myself to sleep. Whether I realized it or not, I must have been praying, begging.

The next morning I got up and flushed those pills down the toilet. No, I was not going to give in nor was I going to give up. I resolved right then that I had the toughest battle of my life ahead of me. I would take each day one at a time, and keep putting one foot in front of the other, to never stop pushing forward.

It took twenty two months for my divorce to be final. A lot longer battle than I would have ever imagined. During those twenty two months my husband bankrupted the company. I eventually had to take on all the personal debt. Financially, I lost everything. But what I won was far more valuable than any dollar amount you could put before me.

My path to freedom began three years ago next month. Even though there were times I thought hope had run out, and although I wasn't aware of it all the time, there was a flame burning deep inside me that never went out. And as it continued to burn, it continued to grow. And so did I.

Today I have a great deal of compassion for my ex-husband, compassion for his pain. I know he is not the man he wants to be. During those fits of rage and battery, something else takes over, something else is in control, and it is deadly. For his current wife, I feel a tremendous amount of fear. Just because I am out, doesn't mean it stopped happening. It just stopped happening to me. Will I turn on the TV one day and hear of another death as a result of domestic violence? Will that woman be the woman that took my place?

> *Bess knew that her marriage to Cole had cost her everything. It had broken her financially, taken her spirit, and raped her soul. But she now knew that God had given it all back to her. In His tremendous love He had given her life back. She would be forever grateful.*

I am not here to win your sympathy towards me. I am only one story. I am here to ask for your support. This is a dangerous problem of epic proportion. These women could be your daughters, today or tomorrow. And to some of you they are today, to some of you, you are the victim today. Some of you are the abuser. Of course, death is not the intent, but deaths are occurring, and it could be you or someone you love.

If you know, or even suspect, of a situation, do something. Do not look the other way or take the "it's none of my business" attitude. It *is* your business. God gave us all a responsibility to each other, to help and to protect.

The victim may feel she is trapped. She is not. There is always, always hope. Never, ever give up."

Bess sat down; almost numb, telling herself you really did it! Wow!

Donna adjourned the meeting. Bess reached down to pick up her purse and when she looked back up she could not believe what was before her. That sea of people was lined up in front of her and around the room. Bess was overwhelmed and breathless. Men and women came up to her and thanked her for coming, for sharing her story, for her courage. Bess couldn't believe what was happening. But she knew in that moment that she had helped someone, the same help that God had so graciously shown her.

"He restores my soul"
Psalm 23

CPSIA information can be obtained at www.ICGtesting.com
Printed in the USA
LVOW10s1117250315

431707LV00001BB/8/P